Work and Vocation through the Lens of Ecclesiastes

Work and Vocation through the Lens of Ecclesiastes

GILBERT SOO HOO

RESOURCE *Publications* • Eugene, Oregon

WORK AND VOCATION THROUGH THE LENS OF ECCLESIASTES

Copyright © 2021 Gilbert Soo Hoo. All rights reserved. Except for brief quotations in critical publications or reviews, no part of this book may be reproduced in any manner without prior written permission from the publisher. Write: Permissions, Wipf and Stock Publishers, 199 W. 8th Ave., Suite 3, Eugene, OR 97401.

Resource Publications
An Imprint of Wipf and Stock Publishers
199 W. 8th Ave., Suite 3
Eugene, OR 97401

www.wipfandstock.com

PAPERBACK ISBN: 978-1-6667-3107-1
HARDCOVER ISBN: 978-1-6667-2320-5
EBOOK ISBN: 978-1-6667-2321-2

Quoting previously published materials in this work fall within "fair use." All quotes used are acknowledged and credited in the associated footnotes.

All Scripture quotations, unless otherwise indicated, are taken from the Holy Bible, New International Version®, NIV®. Copyright ©1973, 1978, 1984, 2011 by Biblica, Inc.® Used by permission of Zondervan. All rights reserved worldwide. www.zondervan.com. The "NIV" and "New International Version" are trademarks registered in the United States Patent and Trademark Office by Biblica, Inc.®

Scripture quotations marked ESV are from The ESV® Bible (The Holy Bible, English Standard Version®), copyright © 2001 by Crossway, a publishing ministry of Good News Publishers. Used by permission. All rights reserved.

Scripture quotations taken from the (NASB®) New American Standard Bible®, Copyright © 1960, 1971, 1977, 1995, 2020 by The Lockman Foundation. Used by permission. All rights reserved. www.lockman.org

09/30/21

Contents

Preface vii

Acknowledgments ix

Abbreviations xi

Chapter 1   Introductory Matters   1

Chapter 2   Career versus Vision   16

Chapter 3   Professional Colleagues as Neighbors   38

Chapter 4   Pursuit of Balance   54

Chapter 5   Marketplace Incongruities   67

Chapter 6   Role of the Church   85

Chapter 7   Reflection and Recommendations   101

Bibliography   111

Preface

Over the years of ministry, my conviction has grown that marketplace Christians, comprising the vast majority of believers, occupy a strategic place in the kingdom. Their presence in the workplace, to which pastors and other professional Christian workers may not have access, represent possibly the only light and salt their coworkers will experience. If their colleagues will not go to church or other Christian gatherings of their own volition, then believers, as Christ's emissaries, must go to work not just to fulfill their professional responsibilities but also to incarnate the gospel as compelling witnesses.

Like pastors who train in seminary and as interns, marketplace Christians need equipping. Churches usually provide adequate spiritual nurturing through preaching Christ and him crucified (1 Cor 2:2). But I believe churches can equip their members even more if they consider marketplace-specific discipleship through the various venues available. Those could include preaching and teaching, small groups, mentoring, and coaching that addresses issues members face at work.

Additional resources in the form of conferences, seminars, parachurch initiatives, and literature such as the present volume augment what churches can offer. In this regard, I offer another lens, or perspective, on work and vocation, that from the wisdom literature, particularly Ecclesiastes. Other studies utilize the lens of the creation mandate and the kingdom perspective, both of which I have profited from.

Preface

But why Ecclesiastes? First, the writer covers the topic of work and labor, which encompass all meaningful work and not just employment in the traditional sense. Second, a major objective of wisdom is enabling the reader to succeed in life. The wisdom literature of the Bible nuances success as alignment with God's will, purpose, and teaching in order to revere him. Third, as the wisest of men, the writer offers insights, admonition, and warnings from his own observations and work experience to infuse wisdom into the life of the reader so that they too may live and work wisely.

Acknowledgments

This book began as a seed planted in the fertile soil of my students who enrolled in the course Theology of Work and Vocation at Singapore Bible College. Over the years, the ideas and convictions germinated and grew. What really spurred the maturation of my views was a semester where I taught two separate sections of the course, one composed primarily of students who desired in-depth study of the Bible but who would remain in the marketplace and the other consisting of students preparing for the pastorate. The former group resonated with my point of view, but the latter group struggled. The first section appreciated affirmation of their sacred duty in the workplace; the second could not quite free themselves from the traditional dichotomous view of the sacred and the secular. But I am grateful to both groups that semester and to all the students who have taken that course for sharpening my thinking and clarifying my conclusions.

Closer to home, I am proud of my children, Weiki and Winyan, as they pursue their respective careers. They experienced some of the incongruities I write about and still managed to advance in their chosen fields. Finally, I acknowledge my wife, Ming, as one of the hardest-working professionals and a great inspiration to me. Even at home she is hardworking. Thank you, Lord, for my family.

Abbreviations

AB	Anchor Bible
BLS	Bible and Literature Series
BSac	*Bibliotheca sacra*
CTM	*Concordia Theological Monthly*
DBSJ	*Detroit Baptist Seminary Journal*
GJ	*Grace Journal*
IVP	InterVarsity Press
JSOTSup	Journal for the Study of the Old Testament Supplement Series
NT	New Testament
NICOT	New International Commentary on the Old Testament
NZSTR	*Neue Zeitschrift für Systematische Theologie und Religionsphilosophie*
OT	Old Testament
RevExp	*Review and Expositor*
SBC	Singapore Bible College
SBL	Society of Biblical Literature
SOTSMS	Society for Old Testament Studies Monograph Series

CHAPTER 1

Introductory Matters

Previous authors use the creation mandate or the kingdom perspective to understand work and vocation.[1] Actually, both approaches together span the full extent of human history from creation to re-creation. Other authors address the integration of faith and works.[2] Still others deal with ethical issues in the marketplace.[3] All these writings represent different ways to examine the subject of work and vocation. No one approach exhausts the subject. In fact, viewing the matter from different angles gives a fuller appreciation of the issues involved. So, I offer yet another set of lenses to sharpen our focus.

WISDOM APPROACH TO VOCATION

The proverbial journey of life can take unexpected turns. We make adjustments and perhaps reconcile in our mind that what we had hoped for as a career would have to be changed as reality asserts

---

1. Stevens views the creation mandate within the broader concept of the covenant mandate that spans creation and new creation (*Other Six Days*, 89–104). For the kingdom perspective, see Witherington, *Work*, but Stevens also discusses it (*Other Six Days*, 163–89).

2. See, for example, Burchell and Robin, *Great Workplace*; Miller, *God at Work*; Fraser, *Marketplace Christianity*; and Hillman, *9 to 5 Window*.

3. Hill documents real-life examples in *Just Business*. But all anecdotes are based on American enterprises. Also see Stevens and Ung, *Taking Your Soul to Work*.

itself. We don't have the requisite giftings or aptitudes. Or we discover something else about ourselves. Circumstances prove nonnegotiable. Or parents exercise profound influence, as my father once did in steering me away from a proposed career as a professional stargazer to something more earthbound—engineering, his field.

The experience of the unexpected, of disappointment, of frustration, or of barriers can be daunting, creating within us negative emotions and perplexity. As Christians we may have committed our lives to the Lord and prayed for guidance. We prefer that the direction of our lives has clarity and the path be smooth without heart-pounding drama. I experienced the latter when I quit my job and enrolled in seminary. I had no real idea what seminary was about or a clear vision of future ministry. The well-planned, orderly life path vaporized.

Here the wisdom literature can guide us in calibrating our perspective and expectations. The Bible features three wisdom books—Job, Proverbs, and Ecclesiastes.[4] Of the three writings, which might more closely reflect the situations we face in life and the marketplace? Have we wondered about a given work situation, relationship with colleagues or clients, or the progress of our careers? Do things seem puzzling or confusing, or not make sense? Have we suffered from an unreasonable boss or toxic work environment? Are we shackled with unrealistic projects or deadlines? Do we wrestle with moral dilemmas at work? Do we face the uncertainty of not seeing the significance of our work relative to the organization's goals? Are we pondering whether our career path is the "right" one?

The Particular Lens of Ecclesiastes

Whereas all three wisdom books can provide useful advice, direction, and perspective, the differences between them can inform our choice about which of the three to read more closely, depending on our particular circumstance. Of special consideration is

---

4. For a convenient one-volume treatment of all three books, see Alter, *Wisdom Books*.

our difficulty in discerning God's involvement with our work and career. Traditionally, Proverbs has been viewed as depicting life as fairly simple and predictable—do the right thing and God will bless; do the wrong thing and face the expected consequences. But a closer reading reveals complexity rivaling that of the other two wisdom books.[5] Actually, the concept of retributive justice comes from the Deuteronomistic teaching in Deut 28–30. In contrast, Job sees life as not simple and predictable. The righteous suffer, upsetting the retributive justice evident in his understanding. Mystified, Job protests to God, demanding answers. However, in the frames that begin and end the book of Job, chapters 1–2 and 42:7–17,[6] the big picture emerges to explain the incongruities in Job's life, although Job never acquires the big picture to which only we readers are privy. Eventually, God rebukes and exonerates Job.

In sharp contrast to Proverbs and Job, Ecclesiastes complains that life does not make sense at all. Are there any benefits for the righteous or wise when they, along with the wicked and foolish, face the same fate—death? Is this life meaningful, then? Ecclesiastes views God as inaccessible. Unlike Job, Qohelet[7] does not seek an audience with God in order to rectify the perceived injustice. In that sense, Job is much more hopeful than Qohelet. Job never gives up, but Qohelet seems resigned to his fate. For the most part, Ecclesiastes asks an unanswerable question: "How does one explain the incongruities of life?" But life is not totally hopeless and contradictory,[8] because Qohelet does not have the final word on

---

5. Hatton, *Contradiction*, 5–11. Hatton finds contradictions, paradoxes, and incongruities in Proverbs. In his chapter "Provocative Contradiction: The Acts–Consequence 'Construct,'" Hatton cites examples of the problematic relationship between human activities and their corresponding consequences (*Contradiction*, 83–116). There is not always a clear and direct relationship between human deeds and divine intervention.

6. Hartley, *Job*, 538–45.

7. Qohelet is a transliteration of the Hebrew participle used substantively to refer to the main speaker of Ecclesiastes and denotes "assembler" or "teacher," although uncertainty lingers about the meaning of the term. See McCabe, "Message of Ecclesiastes," 85n2.

8. For the apparent contradictions in Ecclesiastes, see Fox, *Time to Tear Down*, 1–4.

the matter. Like the book of Job, Ecclesiastes also features a frame before and after the body of Qohelet's musings; in particular, the epilogue provides the theological framework for the whole book.[9] These final words function as an interpretative lens for reading the main body.[10] Enns offers a contemporary version for the epilogue: "Qohelet is wise, my son. Listen carefully. But this is not all there is. Qohelet's words, as wise as they are, are not the final word on your existence as a follower of God."[11]

In Eccl 12:11, the frame narrator likens the words of the wise to goads and their collected sayings to embedded nails used by a shepherd. Goads and nails prod sheep by causing pain, so the words of the wise and their collected sayings push people to better conduct.[12] Next follows a warning (Eccl 12:12) not to continue investigating the absurdities of life because one cannot do more than what Qohelet has done (Eccl 12:9–10).[13] Then comes the conclusion: "The end of the matter; all has been heard. Fear God and keep his commandments, for this is the whole duty of man." (Eccl 12:13 ESV). This concluding admonition provides the context to read Qohelet's observations about the struggles of life. The frame narrator does not disagree with Qohelet but qualifies those struggles from the perspective of one's duty to God. Everyone must struggle with the vicissitudes and the sometimes puzzling and unpredictable aspects of life and work; but a more fundamental principle is operative—one's duty to God in acknowledging his authority. Finally, Eccl 12:14 provides the reason for the admonition—God will bring

---

9. For my discussion on the theological framework, I find Enns very helpful (*Ecclesiastes*, 7–16, 110–16).

10. Because the frame views Qohelet in the third person, commentators posit more than one voice or perspective for Ecclesiastes. See, for example, Fox, who identifies several distinct personas or voices: Qohlet as reporter and observer, the frame narrator, and possibly the epilogist, who distances himself from Qohelet—the speaker of the body of the book—to provide a more traditional stance (*Time to Tear Down*, 363–75).

11. Enns, *Ecclesiastes*, 110.

12. Fox, *Time to Tear Down*, 354–55.

13. Enns, *Ecclesiastes*, 113–14.

every work into account, a future judgment.[14] Thus, Ecclesiastes exhorts us to face life's incongruities—maybe not fully understanding and even groaning—and to accept our lot by doing our work, enjoying whatever fruit we may gain, and all the while to fear God and to obey his expressed will.

Ecclesiastes identifies four factors that complicate life:

1. God's seemingly arbitrary actions,
2. the inevitability of death,
3. sin,
4. and disappointed expectations in life.[15]

God seems inaccessible, with us not being able to gain an audience to dispel our perplexity. As we read Ecclesiastes, we get the impression that even Qohelet, imbued with wisdom, struggles to understand God and his ways.

Disappointed Expectations in Life

The disappointments in life can make living, working, and pursuing vocation difficult, stressful, and frustrating. We want to know the reason for and ultimate cause of such hardship.

As we trace God's purpose and work through Ecclesiastes, we uncover a number of things. First, by implanting eternity into the heart (Eccl 3:11), God makes humans capable of sensing a bigger picture of reality than what they can comprehend.[16] This limitation keeps humans in their place, confined to the here and now and realizing that God transcends their finite world.[17] Hence, people should make the most of this life (Eccl 3:12). Then Eccl 3:13 lists three

---

14. Longman regards this divine accounting as eschatological (*Book of Ecclesiastes*, 283).

15. Danker, "Pessimism of Ecclesiastes," 9.

16. The term "eternity" may mean the world and darkness (or possibly ignorance or secret) (Crenshaw, *Ecclesiastes*, 97). But, as Ogden observes, the temporal idea fits the context (*Qoheleth*, 59–60). Instead of moments of time as in Eccl 3:1–8, "eternity" refers to something that transcends those moments.

17. Longman sees this human finiteness as a source of frustration (*Book of Ecclesiastes*, 121).

things associated with this life—eating, drinking, and finding satisfaction with work—rather mundane and not at all grand. Given the overall negative tone of the context, this statement sounds like resignation—this is the best that people can hope. With "this is the gift of God" concluding Eccl 3:13, satisfaction in one's toil depends on God enabling them to achieve success.[18] If we harbor big dreams, we may be in for big disappointment. But Ecclesiastes speaks to our disappointments, setbacks, and puzzling situations in life and work.

With reference to work, the writer clearly states that humanity should strive to see the good in all their labor. But our success depends on God. The epilogue assures us that God cares about our toil because he will judge our works (Eccl 12:14).

The expression "all their toil" (Eccl 3:13b) includes all purposeful activities. Then I suggest that we paraphrase Eccl 3:13 as "Everyone should eat and drink and see the good in their vocation. It is a gift of God." Enns offers "the whole duty of man" as an alternative to "everyone."[19] With this understanding, vocation is God's gift to us so that we may experience the satisfaction of completing the work given to us.

Yet, other verses threaten to turn our optimism into pessimism. In rapid succession, we encounter Eccl 1:13b ("It is a horrible occupation God gave to humanity to be concerned"), Eccl 1:14 ("I see all the works under the sun, and behold, all is *hebel*"), Eccl 2:11 ("I considered all my works with trouble I labored to do; and behold all is *hebel*, and there was no benefit under the sun"), Eccl 2:17 ("I hate life because the work done under the sun is horrible to me; indeed all is *hebel*"), ›and Eccl 2:18–21 (which speaks of the frustration of having to leave the fruit of one's labor to someone else after death).[20]

---

18. Weeks regards "gift" as "payment" for work done (*Ecclesiastes and Skepticism*, 73n58). But Longman prefers "gift" because God grants the opportunity and attitude to be able to eat, drink, and enjoy the fruits of one's labor (*Book of Ecclesiastes*, 122). Similarly, see Seow, *Ecclesiastes*, 173. Enns proposes "assigned" (*Ecclesiastes*, 10).

19. Enns suggests "the whole duty of man" as a substitute for "everyone" in Eccl 3:13 in view of the same expression in 12:13 as a "mild corrective" to the pessimism of the book in general (*Ecclesiastes*, 7–16).

20. All the biblical citations in this paragraph stem from my own translation

Compounding our predicament, we read in Eccl 3:16–20 that our fate is no different than that of beasts—death. Indeed, all is *hebel* (Eccl 3:19f). *Hebel* conveys three nuances—insubstantiality, transience, and, foulness.[21] "Insubstantiality" refers to something that appears substantive and promising but fails to deliver, resulting in deep disappointment. "Transience" alludes to the brevity of life. And "foulness" speaks of injustice and even perversion. Hope in one's work morphs into disappointment when what appears promising fails to meet expectations—insubstantiality. The inevitability of death looms heavily when one looks into the future—transience. And life can be unfair—foulness. Thus, this book conditions us to expect disappointment, a relatively brief career, and the unfairness of circumstances.

Vocation: Mission Impossible?

Ecclesiastes is more theological than anthropological because the emphasis is on God being in control and humanity obeying his will.[22] We do so by living in the present and finding satisfaction in our work (Eccl 3:12–13). This is his gift to us (Eccl 3:13c). The future is beyond our grasp and control (Eccl 3:22c; 6:12b; 7:14d; 8:7; 10:14b). Today, the here and now, is our stewardship.

These four complicating factors in life—an inscrutable God, the inevitability of death, sin, and the disappointments of life—make any pursuit of vocation appear impossible. How can we muster the courage and conviction to move forward in our life trajectory?

Ecclesiastes 7:14d declares the difficulty of discerning one's future. The better tactic, then, is to focus on the present. One possible implication may be that we can think about the future, but we have no assurances. Our future rests with God. What he determines will happen accordingly; and we ought to accept our lot. But even in the present, we will experience good and bad days. If we prayerfully beseech him to answer our questions and concerns, he is not obligated

---

to better bring out the pathos.
21. Miller, *Symbol and Rhetoric*, 152.
22. Seow, *Ecclesiastes*, 54–60.

to do so. Not surprisingly, we may wrestle with our careers and lives, be perplexed about the apparent arbitrariness of things, and feel discouraged. We can be doing all the "right" things and still suffer and be confused (Eccl 7:15). The writer of Ecclesiastes calls this *hebel*, or injustice and senselessness. Things just don't add up. From our vantage point, things seem topsy-turvy (Eccl 8:14, 16–17), but not from God's perspective.

At this juncture, we may feel confused and unsteady. Thankfully, Ecclesiastes ends with an unequivocal command: "Fear God and keep his commandments, because this applies to every person" (Eccl 12:13b-c, NASB). This injunction captures the essence of our vocation. If we obey, we fulfill our vocational calling. Qohelet mentions work but does not specify what the labor entails. Having different backgrounds, training, aptitudes, giftings, and opportunities, how each of us pursues our vocation can differ. But all of us should fear and obey God.

God gives us the gift of work over which we can find satisfaction (Eccl 3:13; 5:19). But he does not promise a trouble-free life, devoid of plot twists. Work is still taxing. We may experience frustration with our mission and even with God. We may be plagued by uncertainty. But in the end, we can review what we have gone through and discern God's intervention.

By not allaying the hard-edged aspects of life, Ecclesiastes conditions us to be resilient. Life and mission are not impossible. We may stumble, but we will not fail by heeding the admonition of our whole duty in life—fear God and keep his commandments. And his commandments are two: love God with our whole being and love our neighbor as ourselves.

VOCATION AS A GENERAL CONCEPT

Since a number of writers have covered the general concept of vocation,[23] I make brief mention of it to provide background. Tak-

---

23. For example, Badcock, *Way of Life*, 1–31, 71–142; Veith, *God at Work*, 13–164; Schuurman, *Vocation*, 17–181; Garber, *Visions of Vocation*, 13–238; Kroesbergen, "Static Imagery of Vocation," 90–95; and Bock and Del Rosario, "Table Briefing," 235–43.

ing the two greatest commandments as our starting point—loving God with our whole being and loving our neighbor as ourselves (Matt 22:37-40 and Mark 12:29-31)—we see the totality of God's will for us summarized. Easy to remember, this vocational mandate proves difficult in practice. In specific situations, we want to know the most effective approach to fulfilling these edicts. We pray for guidance but have no infallible Urim and Thummim.

As Kroesbergen suggests, another way to view vocation assumes God's perspective, his plan which we seek to uncover but which remains hidden as we decide what to do.[24] We cannot consult with God in the sense that he will specifically point out one path to follow to the exclusion of any other. Instead, we feel our way forward, perusing the Scriptures, praying, meditating, and consulting wise counselors. Yet all the while, God guides and intervenes. Only later in looking back do we discern that God had been involved all along (the classic example being Joseph, Gen 50:15-20). All this presupposes that we conscientiously seek his will. However, there may be some latitude where several possibilities remain open and choosing any one would still be within his will.[25] We weigh the options, considering the advantages and disadvantages of each. Wisdom narrows the choices to the spiritually expedient.

But not having absolute certainty about God's specific purpose for us is not a concession to postmodernism. Postmodernism avows that no one can know for certain what meaning and purpose there exist for life. We affirm, however, that God assigns meaning and purpose. We further affirm that God has set the standard of morality as revealed in the Scriptures.

Vocation as a calling to live life from the divine perspective emerges in practical ways through our daily plans and activities, including work.[26] Every believer is called to love, faith, and hope. We can view vocation from the broader perspective of honoring God with our lives and also from the more specific perspective of particular occupations—engineer, lawyer, teacher, IT specialist,

---

24. Kroesbergen, "Static Imagery of Vocation," 92-94.
25. Friesen and Maxson, *Decision Making*, 137-423.
26. Bock and Del Rosario, "Table Briefing," 236.

housewife—that we do for a certain period of time. For example, a friend of mine began his career as a staff engineer before joining a large hotel chain as an itinerant inspector of the hotel's physical facilities in its far-flung localities and eventually being promoted to become a senior engineer with significant management responsibilities with less direct involvement in technical operations. Throughout his career, he was an engineer working for various corporations that called for different skill sets. He used his analytical abilities, pragmatism, and even language skills as the company's representative in a foreign country. Pursuing our vocation involves the intentional (self-evaluation, planning, preparing, seeking) and the circumstantial (opportunities, recognition by others). God's intervention may be seen in our aptitudes (how he wired us), our giftings (how he empowered us), our motivation and drive (how he stirred us), and our progress (how he provided opportunities and enabled us to succeed). An external observer may explain our successes as our good fortune or as due to our innate ability. Discerning God's presence and acknowledging him require faith. So, vocation is also a call to live by faith.

In a conversation between Darrell Bock, senior research professor in New Testament Studies and executive director of cultural engagement at Dallas Theological Seminary, and Steven Garber, founder and principal of the Washington Institute for Faith, Vocation, and Culture, Garber stated, "Faith shapes vocation, which shapes culture for everyone everywhere."[27] He speaks of the impact our vocation can have on the world, in particular the culture within which we live and work. Then Bock follows with a question: "Therefore, recognizing that God has placed each person in a particular place of employment for a certain time, how should a Christian live out the general calling to honor God in the context of a specific workplace?"[28]

This question prompted the writing of this book. One of my fundamental objectives is to affirm readers in so-called secular careers that their potential to honor God and to impact society is at

---

27. Bock and Del Rosario, "Table Briefing," 237.
28. Bock and Del Rosario, "Table Briefing," 237–38.

least as great as that of vocational ministers, if not greater. Over 90 percent of church members consist of marketplace Christians, most of whom will never enter full-time vocational ministry. It cannot be that they missed out on God's leading in their lives and careers if they do not become pastors or missionaries. Yet, they are ministers of the gospel beyond the walls of the church through their careers and occupations.

OUR VOCATION: EXPERIENCING AND DISPENSING COMMON GRACE

Garber further states: "It's through our vocations that we are to take up this work of common grace for the common good."[29] Scripture depicts God's grace as common and special. Psalm 104:5–32 offers the classical expression of God's common grace in a well-run universe where he provides for all the creatures. Special grace is salvific, conveyed by the gospel and incarnated in Christ Jesus. Since both kinds of grace come from God and manifest his character and benevolence, glorifying him, grace—whether common or special—is sacred. Our enjoying the natural beauty around us, I believe, fulfills God's intent, especially if we acknowledge the creator of beauty. My Singaporean neighbors have ready access to some pristine beaches that do not require air travel and that offer a weekend adventure.[30] Maybe because I grew up where winter can be harsh, I still get a thrill every time I see flowering shrubbery year-round in Singapore, in spite of having been here several years. Even though the Mass Rapid Transit (MRT) suffers the occasional breakdown, it still represents a part of the highly functional infrastructure here. Ultimately, common grace encompasses both naturally occurring and man-made wonders that make life sustainable and pleasant. God provides the sun and rain to the just and unjust (Matt 5:45b). That is common grace; it pertains to the here and now, to this life.

Our vocation calls for us to experience and to dispense common grace in the marketplace. We work hard, giving our best to

29. Bock and Del Rosario, "Table Briefing," 238.
30. Hunter, "10 Unexplored Islands."

the organization—colleagues, clients, contractors, stakeholders—so that all may benefit. We benefit too, for work provides us with a livelihood and the ability to support our family. Our labor, directly or indirectly, contributes to the economy and, if ours is a multinational corporation, can have far-reaching implications for international relations. All this appears secular, worldly. But that is what common grace accomplishes and parallels what God does as he blesses the world. Whatever God does is sacred. When we show common grace in the marketplace, we manifest God's grace and so reveal his sacred presence.

Often when Christians consider a call to full-time ministry, they believe that represents the noblest means of contributing to the kingdom. Perhaps. But such a call excludes most Christians. The majority of NT occurences of "calling" relate to salvation or a holy life. This means that believers fulfill their calling through a life dedicated to God by serving others, regardless of profession. Showing common grace by seeking the common good of others, particularly in the workplace, can be the noblest means of advancing the kingdom—something only marketplace Christians can do, since that domain is often off-limits to pastors.

THE APPROACH FOR THE PRESENT INVESTIGATION

Using Scripture's wisdom literature as the lens by which to examine work and vocation, I will mine Ecclesiastes for insights. Doing so recognizes a key characteristic of the book—its honest discussion of the incongruities and even absurdities of life. The author, Qohelet, does not ignore or deny what puzzles him and lies beyond his understanding. Life does not always make sense or happen as expected. Disappointment, frustration, and even grief and anger may weigh heavily on the heart. Life can be complicated and messy, where solutions to problems appear elusive. What applies in life in general can also surface in the marketplace. In fact, work hours constitute a significant part of the typical week, and work-related issues can spill over outside of the office when workers take their work home, not necessarily literally but mentally in the form of worry and tension.

Unlike Deut 28–30, which presents an orderly universe—the righteous receive rewards and the wicked face consequences[31]—Job and Ecclesiastes and even Proverbs with some incongruities depict situations that feature no straightforward solutions for the inquirer. Job never finds out why he suffers because God does not answer his charges of injustice. Instead, God demands that Job acknowledge the vast gulf between them. Unlike Job, Qohelet does not seem to seek an audience with God, regarding him as remote and inaccessible. The closest Qohelet comes to a possible approach to God is when he admonishes those entering the house of God to listen rather than to speak (Eccl 5:1–7). Yet, Qohelet habors a deep reverence for God and regards him as inscrutable (Eccl 3:11c). For both Job and Qohelet, life can be puzzling and inexplicable. Their worldviews are more nuanced and realistic because the righteous are not always blessed and the wicked are not always punished (Eccl 7:15).[32] In this regard, then, the books of Job and Ecclesiastes provide valuable wisdom for the marketplace Christian worker dealing with the complexities of life and work. And since Ecclesiastes specifically addresses the labor with which one engages, I will use that writing as a reference point.

As the writer of Ecclesiastes states: "I set my mind to seek and explore by wisdom about everything that has been done under heaven" (Eccl 1:13a, NASB). This scope includes marketplace pursuits and activities. Being a very wise man, perhaps the wisest in history (Eccl 1:16), Qohelet explores the full breadth of life through experimentation (Eccl 2:1–10) and observation (Eccl 2:11). He records his findings and conclusions for future generations to ponder. He offers sage advice and instruction. Yet, a major motif

31. Watts depicts Israel's rather complex history subsequent to taking the promised land, arguing that the people's habitual rebellion and idiolatry leading to their later deportation to Assyria and Babylon are the predominate reason why they do not experience the simplicity of Deut 28–30 (see "Deuteronomic Theology," 321–36).

32. Brueggemann labels the ambiguity, incongruity, and mystery of God in his dealings with his people as Israel's "countertestimony" in *Theology of the Old Testament*, 317—406.

keeps surfacing to darken the reading experience—"'Meaningless! Meaningless!' says the Teacher. 'Utterly meaningless! Everything is meaningless'" (Eccl 1:2). Stated in Eccl 1:2 and repeated nearly verbatim in 12:8, this refrain forms a grand inclusio to nearly the entire book. The term *hebel*, translated here as "meaningless,"[33] conveys the three different but related nuances of insubstantiality, transience, and foulness.

Book Outline

With the current chapter as an introduction to the use of Ecclesiastes as the particular lens by which to investigate the Christian's stewardship in the marketplace in view of God's two greatest commandments, I briefly present the layout for this book.

Chapter 2 contrasts the concepts of career and vision. Often we think in terms of career as we map out our marketplace trajectory. Although this process proves quite useful as we factor in our aptitudes, giftings, and personal preferences, we really do not differ from people with a humanistic orientation. Instead, we can adopt a vision for our lives as a compass to direct our ambition and activities, including work-related planning. Career focuses more narrowly on our marketplace ambition, whereas vision casts a broader net to embrace all of life, including, but not exclusively, the marketplace.

Chapter 3 adjusts our view of our professional colleagues as neighbors according to Jesus' teaching from that particular parable. The shift in perspective promises to be impactful as we recognize that the very first step toward practicing common grace requires us to regard our coworkers as people who need our love and compassion rather than simply as other clogs in the industrial machine, as objects to be manipulated for personal gain, or as competitors or rivals in a cutthroat environment.

Chapter 4 addresses the often-elusive goal of achieving balance. Striving toward fulfilling responsibilities in each and every significant area of life can prove daunting should any one area

---

33. *Hebel*, although translated as "meaningless," is a noun ("meaninglessness").

threaten to demand more of our time and personal resources to the point of neglect in other areas. As noted earlier, all of life is important to God and hence sacred. We cannot afford to compartmentalize in designating some areas as holy and other areas as profane, because God holds us accountable for how we live in the totality of all our responsibilities.

Chapter 5 discusses the incongruities in life which, to a certain degree, Qohelet brings out in his writings and which appear as contradictions or paradoxes, events that simply do not add up. Such inconsistencies go against expectations and hopes, resulting in disappointment, puzzlement, or something stronger, like anger and questioning God's role in one's life. This latter point contrasts with Scripture's general portrayal of God—an alternative picture of the divine as found in the rest of the Bible.[34]

Chapter 6 brings to the fore the role of the local church, particularly in the lives of its marketplace members. Two distinct but important ministries—the faithful proclamation of the gospel of Jesus Christ, him crucified and raised from the dead, and the more nuanced, workplace-specific support of teaching, guiding, and counseling working members—merit serious consideration by church leaders in positioning their church to effectively prepare its members to face the majority of their week out in the world.

The seventh and final chapter summarizes the discussions of the preceding chapters and offers some general reflection and recommendations.

---

34. Enns, *Ecclesiastes*, 153–54. Enns rephrases Brueggemann's "countertestimony" as "counterpoint."

CHAPTER 2

Career versus Vision

Perhaps the only parallel Moses and I share lies in having multiple careers—he as Egyptian prince, outcast shepherd, and leader of Israel's exodus out of Egypt through the wilderness to the very threshold of the promised land, and I as marketplace worker, pastor, and then theological educator. Neither one of us planned it that way. Circumstances with God orchestrating moved us from one career to another.

Relying on God's sovereign intervention, however, should not excuse us from taking responsibility for the direction and progression of our career(s). It is not a case of "que sera, sera" ("what will be, will be"), in spite of the expression being the title of a popular Doris Day song in the mid-1950s. But we are not left to fend for ourselves or be totally vulnerable to a trial-and-error approach. A number of resources provide guidance for assessing one's career and deciding whether a change may be called for.[1] We can also consult experts or mature counsel for advice. Practical considerations enter into the picture along with a sanctified pursuit of God's will in prayer. After all, the greatest commandment calls for exercising our minds and not just our hearts in loving our God. Indeed, the gift of Scripture requires spiritually conditioned and enabled readers with "the mind of Christ" (1 Cor 2:16). And what better source of wisdom can we

---

1. For example, Thurrott factors in COVID-19 in advising about potential career changes ("7 Questions").

find than the canonical wisdom literature, particularly Ecclesiastes, which focuses on difficult situations "on the ground"?

By "career," people usually mean a job or series of related jobs in a particular field of endeavor over a significant portion of one's life—for example, a career in engineering, medicine, or athletics. Regardless of the field, we desire some kind of progression following a particular migration path which may feature a series of job changes that takes us ever closer to realizing our career objective. But if we desire to incorporate the concept of vocation into our working lives, we need to look at the big picture. We need to embrace a vision.

EMBRACING THE BIG PICTURE

As discussed in the previous chapter, vocation encompasses all of life with all its attendant activities. In this regard, "work" assumes a much broader scope that includes marketplace toil, fulfillment of domestic chores and parental responsibilities at home, involvement in community service and a local church, and other pursuits, whether hobbies, personal projects, or social engagements. Biblical vocation finds expression in the pursuit of the two greatest commandments. Seen from this perspective, we regard life as relational—relating to God and to neighbor. Indeed, all the commandments and precepts in Scripture pertain to relationships. Of the ten commandments, the first four safeguard the relationship with God and the final six address relationships with neighbors. The characteristic of love looks different in how we love God and how we love neighbor. In the former case, we love God through total consecration to his glory and service; obeying his commandments and edicts; submitting to his lordship; worshiping him in spirit and in truth; and maintaining a continuous dialogue through interactive worship, prayer, and devotional activity. We love neighbor through identifying their needs and, when able, meeting those needs in practical ways; interceding for them; providing companionship through fellowship, empathy, and sharing common interests; offering advice and guidance as appropriate; and grieving with those who suffer loss. Both types of relationships are tangible, heartfelt, and potentially sacrificial. The very essence of love is sacrifice, as God demonstrated on the cross.

Possessing a clear vision, or rather, being possessed by a clear vision, functions as a reference point in orienting our lives and activities so that everything aligns with the vision. Then we can achieve coherence in all areas where each area complements rather than conflicts with other areas. This point will resurface when we address the pursuit of work-life balance. A relevant example, discussed in more detail in the following chapter, concerns regarding our colleagues in the workplace as neighbors. By doing so, we do not differentiate professional coworkers from someone living next door or down the hall of our apartment complex. All merit our care. Of course, a good deal of our interaction with colleagues reflects the professional relationships necessary in the collaboration toward completing a project.

Our vision serves as a yardstick in evaluating any future undertaking for its potential in facilitating our relationships with God and neighbor. Our motivation to pursue any enterprise should be driven by the desire to fulfill the vision. If our vision centers on relationship with God and neighbor, we would naturally seek career options which permit us to honor and serve our Lord and to bless our neighbors. Of course, the complexities of life may make weighing the options and arriving at a decision quite difficult and leave us uncertain, as we may not have all the information needed or have full assurance that our calculations are correct. Unanticipated factors may adversely affect our projections.

Thoughts from Ecclesiastes

The largely autobiographical writings of Qohelet, which constitute the bulk of Ecclesiastes, document his career trajectory. He identifies himself as "the Teacher" and the "king over Israel in Jerusalem" (Eccl 1:12). Textual evidence suggests that he may be a two-career person, first ruling as king and later becoming a teacher who reminisces and philosophizes about what he learned as king. Without pursuing his historical identity, I depend on the predominately ahistorical characteristic of wisdom writings, which, with some exceptions, focus on universal truths. Of course, some historical references surface (Eccl 4:13–16; 8:2–6; 9:13–18), but sufficient details that can pinpoint a more precise time frame proves lacking.

Qohelet's description of his grandiose projects (Eccl 2:4–9) do not provide a specific time line. So, we can only conjecture as to the duration of his activities. Obviously, the scale and scope of his plans require the necessary authority and resources that only a ruler possesses. He achieves his ambitious goals but, upon reflection, labels all his efforts as *hebel* (Eccl 2:11b). The ultimate culprit is death and, in due season, he will soon be forgotten (Eccl 2:15–16). He laments the temporary nature of his acquired fame and accomplishments. He must leave them to a successor (Eccl 2:18), worthy or not (Eccl 2:19–21). Here, then, *hebel* connotes transience—life is too short and the spectre of death bears down with irresistible force. To Qohelet, it does not seem fair. He feels robbed, cheated.

But we may puzzle about his perceived quandary—do not all kings reign for a period of time before a successor, typically the son or, in some cases, the daughter, ascends to the throne? But the way he phrases his lament leaves the impression of distance between himself and a possible successor: "I hated all the things I had toiled for under the sun, because I must leave them to the one who comes after me. And who knows whether that person will be wise or foolish? Yet they will have control over all the fruit of my toil into which I have poured my effort and skill under the sun. This too is meaningless" (Eccl 2:18–19). Apparently, Qohelet does not know the identity of his successor or that person's character. Likely, then, that person is not his descendant. But the possibility of a direct descendant becoming the next ruler remains an open issue, as Qohelet may express his lament rhetorically and somewhat abstractly. Yet, should the successor prove worthy, we question whether or not Qohelet would still be so despondent. The thrust of his writing seems to highlight more the transience of his life and career than a successor, although that consideration still matters to him.

He appears to articulate a personal vision with regard to career and life when he states: "I applied my mind to study and to explore by wisdom all that is done under the heavens" (Eccl 1:13a) and "I said to myself, 'Look, I have increased in wisdom more than anyone who has ruled over Jerusalem before me; I have experienced much wisdom and knowledge.' Then I applied myself to the understanding of wisdom, and also of madness and folly" ((Eccl 1:16–17a). His vision and agenda encompass far more than the typical worker pondering career options. With uncommon resources and privileges, and possessing exceptional wisdom and understanding, Qohelet aspires to the lofty goal of comprehending all of life: What is humanly possible to accomplish? What fruit is borne through the exercise of wisdom? What are the implications and consequences of abandoning common sense and logic to pursue something foolish and even crazy? He aims to immerse himself in all the possible human activities that seem worthwhile to him and to experience any gain or loss and any resultant emotions and possible insights.

After a life of experimentation as a king, he draws some philosophical conclusions as a teacher that border on disillusionment. He writes: "I have seen all the things that are done under the sun; all of them are meaningless, a chasing after the wind. What is crooked cannot be straightened; what is lacking cannot be counted" (Eccl 1:14–15). The word "meaningless" (*hebel*) connotes insubstantiality. The inability to alter circumstances, crooked processes or situations, and deficiencies leaves him feeling helpless and hopeless. He struggles to accept his human limitations. That frustration exposes unbounded ambition, the desire to exceed human boundaries. This idea resurfaces later: "He [God] has also set eternity in the human heart; yet no one can fathom what God has done from beginning to end. . . . I know that everything God does will endure forever; nothing can be added to it and nothing taken from it. God does it so that people will fear him" (Eccl 3:11b-c, 14). Having a sense of eternity in the heart implies the capability of realizing that there is a bigger picture than meets the eye, that there is more to reality than what is immediately apparent through the physical senses. That larger picture includes God and his activities, often not observable and transcending human ambition, plans, and activities. Qohelet senses this otherworldly reality. But we must infer what his thoughts and feelings toward this reality might be, since he does not state it explicitly. Likely, he is not simply stating that truth neutrally as a matter-of-fact observation. Rather, it seems that he feels the human limitation weighing heavily without recourse. He cannot understand God and his ways fully. He sees the sharp contrast between himself and God and keenly feels his inadequacy by comparison. His admitting that neither he nor any other human can contribute to God's activities (Eccl 3:14b) could suggest that his attempt to add to or subtract from God's agenda ends in failure and frustration. The negative tone of the context (Eccl 2:11—3:22) supports interpreting Qohelet's statements as expressing disappointment at some deep level. His concluding remark that people fear God may not imply reverential awe but dread and intimidation.

Takeaway 1

What can we glean from Ecclesiastes at this point? First, Qohelet demonstrates self-awareness. He knows his situation and talent. He is a king endowed with superior wisdom. Second, he sees the opportunity to explore the human experience in all its multicolored facets and seizes it. Proactive, he wastes no time and moves forward aggressively. Third, he enjoys spectacular success in the achievement of all his goals. And fourth, he pauses to evaluate his career thus far. Exercising wisdom to identify worthwhile projects, to execute his plans effectively, and then to examine the gains he manages to achieve, he is in the perfect position to assess the significance of his career and life.

Certainly, we too can emulate Qohelet in career planning and execution. We follow his example of evaluating our progress and possible gains. The first step involves self-awareness in asking ourselves personal, probing questions. Who am I and what are my inclinations, aptitudes, gifts, and talents? What am I good at and what do I want to do (seeing personal preference as an indication of inclination and aptitudes)? How might I challenge myself to aspire to significance?

Takeaway 2

All this depicts a rather humanistic approach. The God factor is lacking. Qohelet fails to mention any consultation with God through prayer, Bible reading, and seeking spiritual mentors. The most we can say unequivocally is that he recognizes the requirement of a listening posture when entering the house of God (Eccl 5:1–7). His admonition, however, is too broad and general, leaving too much room for a variety of interpretations. Do we go to listen to whatever God may wish to communicate in a nonspecific way, or do we seek answers to specific prayers and petitions? Or perhaps the listening posture depicts the humility of the worshiper before God, the not daring to place one's own agenda ahead of God's and portraying awed silence before him.

Only when we hear the voice of the frame narrator do we obtain something akin to an all-encompassing vision for life orientation that aligns with the rest of Scripture: "Now all has been heard; here is the conclusion of the matter: fear God and keep his commandments, for this is the duty of all mankind" (Eccl 12:13). The God factor takes center stage and focuses the vision on the relationship with God.

This sharp contrast between Qohelet and the frame narrator makes us wonder whether Qohelet's story deviates from the scriptural norm. It certainly seems that way. He sees nothing positive about his life and work. One observation might explain the contrast. Qohelet's pursuits concentrate on personal profit and enjoyment. Everything revolves around his own personal agenda without expressed thought for the benefit of others. Selfish ambition ultimately leads to an empty life devoid of much meaning. If we seek only our own benefit to the exclusion of the needs of others, we too can end up bemoaning a rather insignificant life. We prove delinquent in our vocation of loving God and our neighbor. We have no compassion for others. And if we align with Qohelet in regarding God as someone remote and unrelatable and someone to fear, more like dread, then how can we possibly love God?

Takeaway 3

However, some linguistic clues suggest that Qohelet's work and life experiences, although focused on personal gain and happiness, serve a larger purpose beyond self-profit. His writings and musings constitute a part of the canonical wisdom literature. Such writings offer instruction, guidance, and warning to readers. Having gained wisdom through living a rather full life and experimenting, Qohelet shares his discoveries and insights with succeeding generations of readers. The first clue comes from his self-identification as "the Teacher" who is also a king (Eccl 1:12; 7:27). Befitting his title and official position, he teaches lessons learned to others with authority. Such lessons carry an imperatival nuance—he expects them to give due diligence to absorbing his teaching and to complying with his admonitions. He does not hold back but conveys even the unpleasant aspects of life and work. Raw at times, his depiction is true, at least from his point of view. Also, in contrast to his use of the first person singular ("I," "myself," "my") that conveys a first-person account and witness, his use of the second person singular ("you," "your") and the imperative addressed to an individual throughout his writings[2] explicitly address the reader. Thus, Qohelet conscientiously positions his recorded musings as a public document to readers, striving to benefit them with his wisdom, observations, and warnings. They do not need to repeat his experiments, and through his warnings, he spares them from his own frustrations and prepares them to face their own challenges and disappointments. Autobiographical and intensely personal, his reflections and insights make for compelling reading with a strong sense of urgency—one cannot afford to ignore his teaching. A number of proverbial statements are sprinkled throughout (e.g., Eccl 3:1, 15; 4:5–6, 9–12; 5:1–7; 7:1–14; 9:4–6, 11–12; 10:1–4, 8–20; 11:1–6, 7–10; 12:1–7). The sheer frequency of occurrences clearly marks Qohelet's writing as wisdom literature, timeless, universal, and authoritative. Even the frame narrator regards him as "the Teacher" who imparts knowledge to the people through "many proverbs" and affirms the truthfulness of his words (Eccl 12:9–10).

---

2. For example, Eccl 5:1-2, 4, 6-7; 7:9-10; 8:3; 9:7-10; 10:4; 11:1-2; 12:1.

Thus, Qohelet's wise sayings appear as his effort to love his neighbor. Lessons he learns the hard way—perhaps spending the bulk of his life gaining those precious insights—he finally records for posterity. Others can benefit from his understanding and conclusions through reading his "memoir" without repeating his efforts and mistakes. Then we surmise that Qohelet's two-career path could well divide along the following timeline: his first career leverages all his prerogatives and resources in exploring and experimenting what wisdom and folly can yield; his second career gathers and analyzes his findings, and then draws conclusions that form the content of his writings. Thus, we may follow Qohelet's own self-designation in labelling his two careers—he pursues ambitious enterprises as king with unsurpassed wisdom, and after completing those projects and spending time reflecting, he instructs the people through many proverbs as teacher. However, this neat division of his life does not necessarily imply that he ceases being king in order to become a teacher. Likely, he continues to be king but his attention focuses more on reflection and instruction in the latter portion of his life.

We do not know with certainty whether Qohelet foresees a two-career path at the beginning and intentionally maps his life's pursuits accordingly. But we can appreciate the logical progression. The first portion forms the necessary foundation for the second. Further, we desire to know if an overarching vision directed Qohelet to embrace two careers. Should we confirm that, we could affirm intentionality rather than happenchance. But again, we cannot say with certainty that he has such a vision.

The Perspective of the Frame Narrator

Two distinct personalities, Qohelet and the frame narrator, give voice to their thoughts. Uncertainty surrounds the question of whether the former knows the latter. But the latter is definitely aware of the former and, in fact, comments on the former, offering a qualified commendation of the former's wisdom but, at the same time, not fully agreeing. Brief and to the point, the frame narrator states the vision his readers should maintain—"fear God and keep his commandments, for this is the duty of all mankind" (Eccl 12:13c). As noted earlier, the two greatest commandments summarize and capture the thrust of all God's commandments. Loving God and neighbor entails the vision that defines our vocation. This vision fills the gap Qohelet leaves open. To be fair, however, Qohelet has a high regard for God, as every mention of the divine acknowledges his sovereign authority over humanity (Eccl 1:13; 2:26; 3:10; 6:2; 7:26; 8:2, 12–13; 9:1), his blessings to them (Eccl 2:24; 3:13; 5:18–20; 8:15), his mysterious ways beyond human comprehension (Eccl 3:11; 7:13–14; 8:17; 11:5), his unchallengeable activities (Eccl 3:14), his role as judge over humanity (Eccl 3:15, 17; 9:7; 11:9; 12:14) and as creator (Eccl 7:29; 12:1, 7), and the reverential attitude due him (Eccl 5:1–7; 7:18; 12:13).

Only when we read both Qohelet and the frame narrator do we have the total picture. Qohelet captures much that describes reality, including its raw edges, without apology. He conditions his readers to face the challenges, disappointments, burdens, and unfathomable aspects of life, and to temper unbridled ambition and expectations. The frame narrator exhorts his readers to find significance in relationships, first with God and then with neighbors. Combined, we have the big picture by which to discern our career path and to assess how faithfully we progress on that path.

HAVING A SENSE OF TIMING

Tracking our career path along the proverbial time line as we progress, we naturally desire to discern the appropriateness of any possible move or transition from job to job and from one career to another career. Having the proper sense of timing optimizes chances of advancing toward our career objectives satisfactorily. Of course, the unexpected may threaten to derail careful planning. No one can claim absolute control over circumstances or anticipate all possible contingencies, although one may strive to be preemptive as much as possible. Later, we will discuss planning, including contingency planning.

Thoughts from Ecclesiastes

Ecclesiastes 3:1–15 contains Qohelet's thoughts on time and the sense of timing. This section begins with a proverb stating a universal truth in verse 1: "There is a time for everything, and a season for every activity under the heavens." All of life—events and processes—are time-bound, located in a specific point in history and having a definite starting point and end point. As the clock continues to run, history progresses. Once the time for an event passes, that event becomes history not to be repeated, as time does not move backwards. And since time does not stop, an event or process cannot linger indefinitely. These realities are all too familiar and hardly warrant stating. But Qohelet states them as he prepares to make his point.

Then he follows with a series of pairs (Eccl 3:2–8), where each pair represents polar opposites. They are birth and death, planting and uprooting, killing and healing, tearing down and building up, weeping and laughing, mourning and celebrating, scattering and gathering, embracing and refraining from doing so, searching and giving up, keeping something and throwing it away, tearing and mending, being silent and speaking, loving and hating, and finally, war and peace. Fourteen pairs of human events and activities in all. An immediate question arises—is this list exhaustive, or representative? It appears to be representative, as we can compose other pairs, such as working and not working, eating and fasting, and being awake and sleeping. Each item of any pair is a typical event or activity common to everyone. None appears exceptional or restricted to certain categories of people based on economic or marital status, gender, age, or some other social grouping. The contrasting pairs suggest mutual exclusivity; only one or the other may occur, but not both simultaneously. However, there may be occasions when neither item of a given pair occurs.

But the real significance of these pairs lies in their timing. Regardless of the particular item, the time of its occurrence may be appropriate or not. For example, in 1 Cor 15:8 Paul refers to himself as someone born abnormally or in an untimely fashion in comparison to the other apostles who witnessed the resurrected

Lord. They saw him Easter morning, the very day of his resurrection. Soon afterwards, hundreds of others saw him. Paul, on the other hand, only saw the Lord long after the Lord's ascension and by a specially arranged revelation, thereby becoming the last and, in his estimation, belated witness. In the same way, should someone suffer an untimely death, we usually mean that the death is tragic and more grievous than normal death. The death is premature, the person having died young. Or, if someone tears down something when they should have built it up, then the consequences can prove quite serious and counterproductive and negatively impact others more than necessary. But tearing down a dilapidated structure because of its instability, for example, would not only be timely but also necessary.

Qohelet follows the list of pairs with a rhetorical question ("What do workers gain from their toil?" [Eccl 3:9]) and then a plaintive statement ("I have seen the burden God has laid on the human race" [Eccl 3:10]). At first glance, these two verses seem to introduce a new topic, but no linguistic clue suggests the transition to another subject. Moreover, Qohelet adds, "He has made everything beautiful in its time" (Eccl 3:11a), which, with "there is a time for everything" (Eccl 3:1a), brackets the intervening verses to confirm that the entire discussion deals with time and timing.

The question of gain or profit from one's toil in the context of timing points to the implied answer: much gain, provided the toil has proper timing. Work done within its appointed time offers the potential of maximum profit. This is the ideal. But perfect timing requires a knowledge only God possesses, as Qohelet infers: "He has made everything beautiful in its time. He has also set eternity in the human heart; yet no one can fathom what God has done from beginning to end" (Eccl 3:11). Perfect timing aligns with the big picture. Only God has the big picture and knows how everything fits together, where each component contributes to the overall scheme. The idea of eternity transcends time and encompasses everything that God does from beginning to end. Since God transcends the bounds of time and history, his beginning and end extends "from everlasting to everlasting" (Ps 90:2c). As the psalmist professes, God always exists; he has no beginning point or end point. All that he has done cannot possibly be comprehended by finite humans. Handicapped, humans can strive to ascertain the appropriate timing for an event or activity, but theirs is only an approximation. God alone knows the correct timing precisely. The burden he imposes on humans relates to them determining the proper time for any event or activity. In a sense, it is an impossible task, limited as they are. They will err either to a larger or lesser degree. They live in an imperfect world. And so, the question of gain from their toil highlights their struggle to do the right thing at the right time.

With some resignation, it seems, Qohelet then states to what humanity can aspire with its limitations: "I know that there is nothing better for people than to be happy and to do good while they live. That each of them may eat and drink, and find satisfaction in all their toil—this is the gift of God" (Eccl 3:12–13). Make the most of the here and now—the philosophy of carpe diem. Live the moment and do not worry about the bigger picture, since worry accomplishes nothing. Taking eating and drinking as a synecdoche for all the activities of life and "all their toil" as any and all kinds of responsibilities that a normal person must fulfill, then Qohelet exhorts his readers to recognize that these normal daily activities and pleasures are a gift from God. Rather than seeking the bigger picture futilely and experiencing frustration, aim for what is within reach. God's gift indicates his will. Humanity needs to know its place and accept it as the divine will.

Implications for Work and Career

Humanly speaking, we cannot discern perfectly the timing needed to optimize career or length of stay in any given job situation. We should try, of course, to determine those given what we understand about our abilities, the available opportunities, and circumstances that make our progress more possible or more difficult. Practically, we do what we can. But the more important consideration rests in the present moment. Are we maximizing our opportunities now? Are we fulfilling our responsibilities to the best of our ability? Do we appreciate the present and enjoy the moment? Do we and our family benefit from the fruit of our labor? Do we discern and seize opportunities to serve the community? God gives us the gift of the present; do we appreciate the gift and maximize its benefits? By being faithful to our stewardship of the present, we honor God.

Qohelet next declares: "I know that everything God does will endure forever; nothing can be added to it and nothing taken from it. God does it so that people will fear him" (Eccl 3:14). We can interpret that statement in the broad sense—God is eternal and all that he does has eternal value and implications. The fact that no one and nothing can alter God's purpose and actions speaks of his sovereign authority and his unchangeable plans. In the narrow sense of the individual, God's gift to each of us to live and act in the here and now can also have eternal consequences. That truth receives confirmation when we consider God's judgment on how we live and act. When Qohelet declares "that there is nothing better for people than to be happy and to do good" (Eccl 3:12), our highest aspirations ought to align with that truth. Are we happy and doing good? But what is the good?

The concept of vocation provides the answer. The good in view of the two greatest commandments connotes excelling in loving God and loving neighbor. Through the template of carpe diem, pursuing loving relationships is a daily activity. Herein we find satisfaction and even joy, a sense of fulfillment, and wholeness as we align with our God-given purpose within the sphere of influence and activity entrusted to us. Significantly, the particular type of toil or work is not identified, leaving the impression that, so long as good occurs, it may not matter to God. Obviously, gainful work to meet needs must be a fundamental criterion.

That inherent flexibility gives us freedom to explore our inclinations, preferences, aptitudes, and talent in order to particularize the job and career. If we do tasks that we enjoy doing and display a talent for, we increase the chances of completing the work effectively and thereby find satisfaction. Then we have accepted God's gift. If we do not do good or find satisfaction in our toil, have we perhaps spurned God's gift?

We may question the apparent naivety of Qohelet's statements here, especially in view of his far-reaching comments elsewhere as he repeatedly laments the meaninglessness (*hebel*) of life.[3] Given the nuance of hebel, Qohelet may be complaining about insubstantiality, transience, or foulness, depending on the immediate context. All three ideas express Qohelet's general view that life is absurd, devoid of meaning or significance, and puzzling, leaving one at a loss in trying to make sense of things. But his thoughts encompass the sum total of life and its overall significance. He strives to understand the big picture and perhaps go beyond human boundaries to glimpse God's eternal workings. But his failed efforts frustrate him and leave him disappointed and even disillusioned. He admits how herculean this enterprise is when he confesses: "When I applied my mind to know wisdom and to observe the labor that is done on earth—people getting no sleep day or night—then I saw all that God has done. No one can comprehend what goes on under the sun. Despite all their efforts to search it out, no one can discover its meaning. Even if the wise claim they know, they cannot really comprehend it" (Eccl 8:16–17). When perhaps the wisest person who ever lived acknowledges his inability to grasp the big picture and God's actions, certainly no one else stands a chance to do better. Thus, the wisest course to take is to accept Qohelet's conclusions and not even attempt what he attempted—to accept one's limitations and the mysteries of God and life. Practically speaking, the appropriate course of action focuses on what lies within the scope and capability of humanity—carpe diem, the present moment, the finite sense of the immediate, the day-to-day.

When Qohelet announces that "everything God does will endure forever; nothing can be added to it and nothing taken from it" (Eccl 3:14b–c), he acknowledges that no one can change the operative principle of carpe diem. God has confined humanity to the present; any attempt to break free from the bonds of finiteness will only result in failure. Satisfaction comes when one contentedly stays within the boundaries God has set. A sharp contrast must remain between God and what only he can do, and humans. When we fear him, we recognize that he alone is God. And at the same

---

3. This word motif appears thirty-five times in Ecclesiastes: 1:2 (4x), 14; 2:1, 11, 15, 17, 19, 21, 23, 26; 3:19; 4:4, 7–8, 16; 5:7, 10; 6:2, 9, 12; 7:6, 15; 8:10, 14 (2x); 9:9 (2x); 11:8, 10; 12:8 (3x).

time, we remember our accountability with regard to how well we live and work within those boundaries (Eccl 3:15).

PLANNING ACCORDING TO ECCLESIASTES

The concept of carpe diem may appear to oppose any effort to project into the future and to plan a course of action. But mapping our career path does not even remotely compare with Qohelet's much more ambitious attempt to understand all of life and the ways of God. Employing his exceptional wisdom, he hopes to delve into the mysteries of the world (he scopes his investigative interests to everything "under the sun or heavens" and not to the heavens above). He begins with an examination of the history of human activity and of the world before concluding: "Generations come and generations go, but the earth remains forever. . . . What has been will be again, what has been done will be done again; there is nothing new under the sun" (Eccl 1:4, 9). World history runs in cycles, repeating over and over again.

Qohelet argues from the natural processes that are observable within his lifetime. That realization qualifies our interpretation of his comments. He himself is human and has only lived a very short time relative to world history. He may have studied the writings of historians and extrapolated from his limited observations to extend his conclusions beyond his direct fact gathering. We may dispute his findings when we recall the worldwide cataclysm of the flood in Noah's day and of the fiery day of the Lord to come (2 Pet 3:6, 10). However, Peter's apologetic addresses the scoffers of the last days who will reject prophecies concerning the Lord's return (2 Pet 3:3–10). In contrast, Qohelet is not a scoffer who rejects the Lord's coming by arguing on the fallacious basis of uniformitarianism. Rather, he laments the human inability to contribute anything truly new that, in his view, represents something significant. He repeats this concept a few times as the human inability to change anything on a monumental scale (Eccl 1:15; 3:14b, 15a-b).

We suspect that Qohelet harbors the ambition to rise above human frailty and limitation to approach God's level. Perhaps we can understand his overreach, given his unequaled endowment of wisdom and royal prerogatives and resources. No human interference or circumstance can oppose his ambitious enterprises. Yet, he laments not making a dent in the natural order of the world.

But when we work on our career plans, we do not seek to change the natural world order. That represents a much more ambitious enterprise than, for example, the series of industrial revolutions we have experienced in recent history.[4] We may change the way we live and do business, but we are not changing the world in some fundamental way.[5]

Carpe Diem and Career Planning

The apparent contradiction between carpe diem (the day-to-day, the immediate present) and planning for one's career—looking into the future, often in terms of years—does not necessarily exist. Qohelet's concept of carpe diem really applies to this life overall, as he makes clear, and not just to any individual moment in time or a particular day, although it can also refer to such a brief period as a single day. After completing his ambitious projects (Eccl 2:4–10), he declares: "Yet when I surveyed all that my hands had done and what I had toiled to achieve, everything was meaningless, a chasing after the wind; nothing was gained under the sun" (Eccl 2:11). We can easily imagine his great projects taking years to complete, at the conclusion of which he expresses dissatisfaction with his favorite motif of meaninglessness, expressed through the word *hebel*, connoting insubstantiality—what initially seems promising is, in

---

4. Klaus Schwab lists four industrial revolutions—water and steam power for mechanized production, electric power for mass production, electronics and information technology for automated production, and the digital revolution that blurs the distinction between the physical, digital, and biological spheres. See "Fourth Industrial Revolution."

5. Of course, some people may point to the threat of global pollution and warming and climate change as a fundamental change. That is a modern problem we have inflicted on ourselves. Then, too, the extinction of certain categories of animals may point to human culpability. But it is unlikely Qohelet had this kind of change that fails to honor the creation mandate (Gen 1:28) in mind.

reality, lacking in true significance. A little later, Qohelet laments that the fruit of his life's work will pass to a successor, worthy or not, when he passes on (Eccl 2:14–23). Then he immediately follows with "A person can do nothing better than to eat and drink and find satisfaction in their own toil" (Eccl 2:24a). This latter piece of advice, which clearly defines the carpe diem philosophy, applies to Qohelet's career of project building. The contrast between this latter statement and his lament immediately preceding it suggests that he himself has difficulty accepting and practicing his own advice. But the important observation to make centers on the fluidity of the scope of carpe diem—the temporary, the here and now, the present moment—which focuses on this life and the limited life span of humans. The concept emphasizes the transience of life. So, one must make the most of this life by finding satisfaction in whatever one does and manages to complete, whether daily chores or projects extending into years. Thus, career planning really seeks to maximize the fruitfulness of one's life in taking advantage of its finite number of opportunities; therein one can experience satisfaction now.

Planning with Multiple Options

As we plan our careers and make projections about our future, we do well to heed Qohelet's advice about planning for future ventures. He reveals himself to be a wise and cautious businessman. He begins with "Ship your grain across the sea; after many days you may receive a return" (Eccl 11:1). Envisioning an ambitious international business transaction, he highlights two realities: "many days"—a figurative expression denoting a significant period of time, open to interpretation (weeks, months, years?)—and the element of contingency. These characteristics clarify the parallel with our career trajectory, which encompasses a lengthy period representing a large chunk of our life span—all our working years—and features the uncertainty of success. Work and life offer no guarantees. Our best plans and preparation may eliminate certain risks but not others. The possibility of the unexpected, the unforeseen, and the general vicissitudes of life interfering with and disrupting our careers prompts caution and qualifies our confidence in moving forward. And so, Qohelet offers sage, practical advice.

"Invest in seven ventures, yes, in eight; you do not know what disaster may come upon the land" (Eccl 11:2). The familiar OT numerical sequence of x, x+1 here does not indicate a specific amount per se but the idea of many with some intensification moving from x to x+1.[6] Qohelet exhorts readers considering a business decision to hedge their bets by having multiple options on the table—the more the better—in case something should occur that threatens the success of the venture. If one plan fails to materialize, alternative plans could effectively circumvent the problem. The best strategy calls for preemptive planning and preparation to avoid catastrophic failure as much as possible. With the options at the ready, the investor must obviously make a relatively quick assessment of the situation and progress of the plan before deciding whether to continue with the plan or replace it with an alternative. This process requires alertness and responsiveness.

Observations of nature and its processes (Eccl 11:3–5) suggest that just as those processes consist of both the predictable (Eccl 11:3) and the mysterious (Eccl 11:5), and just as sloth and distraction prove unproductive (Eccl 11:4), these truisms apply equally well to planning and implementation. Some things may be predictable and other things remain inscrutable. From the human perspective, a certain randomness seems to pervade, which Qohelet attributes to God's mysterious ways (Eccl 11:5b). But one thing proves certain—if people are not diligent and timely in the execution of their plans, they will fail to profit.

Then Qohelet concludes: "Sow your seed in the morning, and at evening let your hands not be idle, for you do not know which will succeed, whether this or that, or whether both will do equally well" (Eccl 11:6). He makes several points worth pondering. First, start early (in the morning) and do not delay planning and implementation. Be proactive because delay may result in failure or disaster. Second, do not rest on your accomplishments but keep working (through the evening). Be ever diligent and focused. Keep thinking

---

6. Davis, "Rhetorical Use of Numbers," 40–48.

about your plans and work. Monitor progress of work carefully and constantly. Continue to do whatever is required. Third, no one can accurately forecast how things will turn out. The hope is that at least one venture succeeds, but it may prove difficult identifying which option will pan out. It would be best if all ventures yield a profitable return. But no one can know for certain. All these considerations are practical, indicating that Qohelet heeds his own advice when he pursues his own projects. Successful, he turns to counsel others. They ought to accept and follow his advice because he has ample experience with a highly successful track record. He knows what he is talking about.

CONCLUSIONS

In the second leg of a two-career trajectory, Qohelet functions as a teacher who documents his investigation into life, work, and wisdom for the benefit of his readers. His scope of consideration, however, goes way beyond the average concern about the immediately assessable—personal needs, work, and the various activities occupying life. Instead, he strives to penetrate into the mysteries of the world and the ways of God. Only partially successful and acutely aware his own finite life span, he laments and bemoans the meaninglessness of the human enterprise. He utilizes the motif of *hebel* to connote insubstantiality, transience, and foulness, the three shackles that restrict him from fully knowing the divine, as he states plaintively: "I saw all that God has done. No one can comprehend what goes on under the sun. Despite all their efforts to search it out, no one can discover its meaning. Even if the wise claim they know, they cannot really comprehend it" (Eccl 8:17). Although he can be numbered among the wise and likely exceeds them all in wisdom, Qohelet refuses to boast of any superior understanding about the realities hidden from humanity. He is honest about his humanity, but he does not like it. His innate abilities do not support his ambitious vision to rise above his shackles.

Reading Ecclesiastes, we, too, may feel the heavy chains that bind humanity, but only if we adopt Qohelet's vision. Fortunately, the frame narrator mitigates Qohelet's frustration, disappointment, and disillusionment, which we would have otherwise experienced, by redirecting us to a vision much more achievable and relational. He points us to our duty to God in fearing him and keeping his commandments, which can be distilled into loving God with our all and loving our neighbor.

We may then wonder what purpose or role Qohelet serves. The contrast between the two men suggests that Qohelet is a foil for readers to compare and contrast with the frame narrator. The former seeks personal pleasure (Eccl 2:1–3) and personal achievement (Eccl 2:4–10) and, upon evaluating the results and net benefits to himself, feels empty (Eccl 2:11). He directs everything to himself, being quite self-absorbed. What does he gain or learn? In the end, he can only state: "For with much wisdom comes much sorrow; the more knowledge, the more grief" (Eccl 1:18). On the other hand, the narrator admonishes his readers to be outward focused, first to God and then to others (Eccl 12:13). He makes no promises but infers that the basis for God judging every action is whether it is good or evil (Eccl 12:14). That basis centers on how well people honor God. We infer further that if we honor God, he will judge our lives and deeds as good. If we fail to honor God, he will judge our activities and accomplishments as evil. We achieve satisfaction if we satisfy God's demands.

Do our vision and career objectives align with God and his purpose? This is not the question Qohelet asks. He asks the wrong question: What is God doing that lies outside of the realm of human comprehension (Eccl 3:11b–c; 8:17)? His question is unanswerable. So, he resigns himself to his human limitations: "I know that there is nothing better for people than to be happy [with their limitations and shortcomings] and to do good while they live. That each of them may eat and drink, and find satisfaction in all their toil—this is the gift of God" (Eccl 3:12–13). If God gives something, accept and enjoy it. If he withholds giving something, it would be futile to pine for it. God sets boundaries; be content within those boundaries, because no one can go beyond them. Qohelet tries to cross the line but fails; he learns his lesson the hard way. Thus, he admonishes his readers—don't bother trying; it's useless.

Career versus Vision

In his pursuits, Qohelet experiences *hebel* in its various hues—insubstantiality, transience, and foulness. Even if we heed the frame narrator's admonition to revere and obey God, we may still experience *hebel* because life can be unpredictable and unfair. Bad things can happen to the best of us through no fault of our own—remember Job. And death is inevitable. As Qohelet states, we must all face God's judgment someday. But unlike Qohelet, let us explicitly entrust our lives, work, and career to God so that he receives the honor, no matter the outcome.

CHAPTER 3

Professional Colleagues as Neighbors

An expert in the law once asked Jesus, "Who is my neighbor?" (Luke 10:29). With his parable as an illustration, Jesus guided the expert to conclude that the Samaritan who showed the victim mercy was the true neighbor. One aspect of this parable serves as my springboard for this chapter. Three men encountered the wounded man because they all traveled along the same road. None of them anticipated what occurred. Upon discovering the prostrate figure, they made a decision—two bypassed the opportunity to help and one stopped out of pity.

The Samaritan's compassion was spontaneous, an immediate response to an unexpected situation. The other two men could not be bothered, perhaps being in a hurry or thinking it too inconvenient or dangerous. In any case, recasting this familiar parable from a physical journey from Jerusalem to Jericho along an isolated portion of the road to a contemporary marketplace situation involving four professional colleagues—each on a journey to complete their work assignments or project, perhaps laboring on the same team—affords us an opportunity to consider coworkers as potential neighbors. Can we view our colleagues in the office as neighbors to whom we owe some responsibility to care?

When we do so, one immediate implication emerges—we do not regard each other as the competition and so play office politics. We do not strive to undermine the other person, either to prevent them from performing well or to make ourselves look better by comparison. We do not harbor envy or jealousy. We celebrate their promotions. And, like the Samaritan, we are alert to possible opportunities to provide assistance when called for. Of course, it depends on ability. The Samaritan had bandages, oil, wine, a donkey, and sufficient funds to house the wounded man at an inn.

A cost accompanies neighborliness—it cost the Samaritan time, money, and a detour from his travels. It may cost us in terms of our KPIs, which may not include being a good neighbor to co-workers. If so, we could suggest including a criterion on teamwork, cooperation, mentoring or instructing, and the like, which can open the door to our practicing relational activities.

Years ago when I joined a technical-support team, I started as the newest and least knowledgeable member. Being the most experienced, knowledgeable, and skilled member, our team leader was in the natural position to teach and guide the entire team, as well as to assign each of us our respective duties. Well, she assigned my scope of responsibilities, but—as I was to later discover—whatever she deemed "dirty work" and hence beneath her, she assigned to me. I did not resent my assignment, because it meant I could learn something new and gain some skills that would contribute to the overall team performance. But I was on my own, with no one to consult should I encounter difficulty. Fortunately, I progressed adequately. Later I learned what everyone else on the team had already known—that our team leader kept all the choice assignments for herself and, to ensure that continued arrangement, refused to convey the necessary knowledge to us for any of us to substitute for her should she become incapacitated. Nor could we advance in our careers. Her attitude and practice ran counter to the professional-colleague-as-neighbor viewpoint. An undercurrent of dissatisfaction and discontent characterized our team, even though we all performed our duties well. But at the same time, none of us could progress beyond our limited repertoire of knowledge and skills.

THOUGHTS FROM ECCLESIASTES

Qohelet contributes to the current discussion with his proverbial depiction of the advantage two people have over a single person (Eccl 4:9–12). The opening verse summarizes the profit available to the partnership: "Two are better than one, because they have a good return for their labor" (Eccl 4:9). Given the general nature of this statement, it also applies to colleagues working in the same organization, especially for those on the same team or in the same department. This proverb assumes a good working relationship featuring mutuality of dependence and trust. Each person carries their load and does not slack in fulfilling their responsibilities. Good communication marked by clarity and consensus of purpose and direction facilitates the partnership.

Sometimes bad things happen at work. Qohelet acknowledges this truth when he writes: "If either of them falls down, one can help the other up. But pity anyone who falls and has no one to help them up" (Eccl 4:10). Again, the generic nature of the statement opens to a wide variety of situations for application. Directing this to the marketplace, we can readily envision a number of circumstances, such as the one I cited earlier about my team leader. I was on my own, with no support from her. She expected me to learn and to fulfill my assigned duties independently. So long as I encountered no major problems, I continued unabated. Occasionally, I ran into a difficulty but fortuitously was able to resolve the matter myself. In fact, my area of responsibility lay beyond her own expertise, so I was really on my own. But if I ran into an obstacle I could not handle, what then? Qohelet laments it as "a pity." But pity does not help; substantial help must materialize or the work cannot be accomplished, adversely affecting the organization and its stakeholders. Ideally, a team consists of members who know enough of each other's area of work in order to lend a hand should one member struggle.

The observation "if two lie down together, they will keep warm; but how can one keep warm alone?" (Eccl 4:11), for obvious reasons, cannot be applied to the workplace literally. However, if we make an emotional analogy, we might reword the saying as "if two huddle together to discuss, strategize, and work on a project as a team, they will mutually encourage one another; but how can one person alone stay encouraged?" Working with others reduces the feeling of isolation and provides an available sounding board to ensure that progress does not deviate from the original objectives. Along another front, this observation might play out in a mentor-mentee relationship, where a more experienced colleague coaches, instructs, and guides a less experienced worker.

Then Qohelet notes: "Though one may be overpowered, two can defend themselves; a cord of three strands is not quickly broken" (Eccl 4:12). We can well imagine someone being overwhelmed when facing a daunting challenge with no ready resources available to facilitate completion of the task and having no one else to consult. The fear of displeasing management should a delay or obstacle prove difficult can generate panic attacks or other emotional upheaval. A close-knit team, however, can at least commiserate, if not discuss the matter with someone, proposing a possible solution and finding mutual encouragement.

This passage views the principle of neighborliness in the workplace as a partnership or team dynamic where two or more coworkers share a vested interest in a common cause, collaborate, support each other—especially when one falters or struggles—and find an emotionally safe haven within the team. When the team succeeds, all share in its rewards. When someone falls, all rally to lift them up. Jesus' parable shows the Samaritan taking the initiative out of pity. He gains nothing from helping the victim, and in fact, it remains uncertain whether the victim recovers enough to acknowledge his benefactor. It does not matter, since the Samaritan seeks nothing in return. But in the marketplace, pity may not be the primary motive, but rather the team's success. If a member cannot fulfill their responsibility, the whole team may suffer. Thus, it behooves everyone to pitch in, if necessary. However, shouldering a colleague's duties in addition to one's own can undermine one's performance and thereby cause resentment which threatens to weaken camaraderie within the team. Thus, it cannot remain a long-term situation. Hopefully, recourse is available to enable the faltering member to rectify any shortcomings and then contribute fully.

Being a Wise Neighbor

But for the Christian worker, compassion would be a key characteristic that can manifest itself through acts of charity. In the corporate world, charity is not a typical feature, unlike, for example, ambition, drive, competitiveness, industry, profit orientation, and opportunism. Of course, the Christian should act and work professionally at the highest levels of competence. But what if they work with or encounter a colleague in need of help? Should they sacrifice something of their own time and energy to assist someone, especially if that is not one of their KPIs? It may be a difficult decision to make. Here, Qohelet's pursuit of wisdom offers guidance. In addition to compassion, the Christian worker needs wisdom to discern opportunities to help, the proper way to engage, and the cost and consequences of intervening. Should they consult with management or act alone?

Qohelet testifies to his exercise of wisdom: "I applied my mind to study and to explore by wisdom all that is done under the heavens" (Eccl 1:13a); "My mind still guiding me with wisdom; I wanted to see what was good for people to do under the heavens during the few days of their lives" (Eccl 2:3b-c); "I saw that wisdom is better than folly, just as light is better than darkness; the wise have eyes in their heads, while the fool walks in the darkness" (Eccl 2:13-14a). Purposefully, he utilizes his mental faculties to investigate and analyze in order to understand and gain insight. He seeks the "good for people to do." "Good" likely signifies "a good return for their labor" (Eccl 4:9b). Wisdom can reduce the threat of insubstantiality—something that seems promising or substantial but, on further examination, proves disappointing or worthless. Wisdom can enable a person to see more clearly the factors affecting a decision or choice and the various options with which they may move forward. A lack of wisdom, in contrast, leaves the fool groping in the dark, clueless and ignorant of the potential dangers hidden from view and incapable of making sound decisions and following through with appropriate action.

Mindful of their professional obligations to the organization and relational responsibility to colleagues, Christian workers exercise compassion and wisdom in order to strike the proper balance. They are accountable to offering their best efforts to their companies so that their own work does not suffer; and they remain alert to coworkers who may need their help. Sometimes doing both proves difficult to achieve and maintain. Short-term assistance may lessen the negative impact to the quality of their own work, but would it be sufficient? If not, are there alternatives, such as others stepping in to distribute the load or finding training for the struggling colleague? And if no option seems viable, can they desist helping with a clear conscience?

Biting the Feeding Hand

Another consideration arises when Qohelet pens: "I hated all the things I had toiled for under the sun, because I must leave them to the one who comes after me. And who knows whether that person will be wise or foolish? Yet they will have control over all the fruit of my toil into which I have poured my effort and skill under the sun. This too is meaningless" (Eccl 2:18–19). He thinks of his successor after he passes on (death occupies his thoughts in Eccl 2:14b–21, where the concluding use of "meaningless," or *hebel*, connotes transience). He worries about the worthiness of the one who inherits the result of all his efforts and continues after him. His concern may trigger within us an analogous thought about the worthiness of the one we help. We pour our energy and time into helping a colleague gain competence. Will our efforts prove worthwhile? Will the one helped perform better as a result or will our labor not have a tangible payoff? Will our colleague even appreciate our assistance? What if they benefit and do better but take the credit which rightfully belongs to us? They may boast that their productivity came solely from their own work. Management may think their turnaround came from them and not be aware of our role. Or should we align ourselves with the Samaritan who harbored no thought of personal benefit or gain? But even if we strive to be altruistic, there is still the matter of foulness, *hebel*'s nuance of injustice (Eccl 3:16).

Instead of becoming angry or embittered, we can ponder Qohelet's philosophical outlook and acceptance of life, whether good or bad. He writes: "When times are good, be happy; but when times are bad, consider this: God has made the one as well as the other. Therefore, no one can discover anything about their future" (Eccl 7:14). The previous verse provides the context for interpretation: "Consider what God has done: Who can straighten what he has made crooked?" (Eccl 7:13). Qohelet recognizes God's sovereign authority in all circumstances, whether he likes it or not. We cannot change things to suit our preferences. Qohelet appears to accuse God of wrongdoing in cases where injustice prevails. Perhaps he is; that may well be his perception. The entire book of Ecclesiastes sans the frames, particularly the epilogue, represents his observations and conclusions about life and work through his experimentation and investigation. He senses that some things lie beyond his observations and thoughts to fully understand, especially God and his ways and deeds (Eccl 3:11c; 8:17). His worldview is bounded to things "under the sun/heavens."[1] He finds his physical senses restricting his observations. And he realizes that a bigger picture resides completely outside of his grasp. His statement that God "has also set eternity in the human heart; yet no one can fathom what God has done from beginning to end" (Eccl 3:11b-c) depicts God enabling humans to be aware that there is more than meets the eye, that a reality exists beyond human comprehension. Acutely sensitized to his human limitations, Qohelet feels frustration. He is not content with his human finiteness but has no choice but to accept his humanity. From his human vantage point, he thinks God is the one responsible for the good and bad things people experience. He cannot explain God's rationale—that is, the *why* question has no ready answer. Thus, he resigns himself to accept whatever happens, since there is nothing he can do about it. That point of view, then, is what he recommends for his readers to accept. We may not like what happens at work—decisions by management, office politics, or a colleague we have helped but who fails to appreciate our efforts. We do not understand or like it. But we cannot do anything about it. So, accept it. Qohelet offers practical advice.

1. Eccl 1:3, 9, 13–14; 2:3, 11, 17–20, 22; 3:1, 16; 4:1, 3, 7, 15; 5:13, 18; 6:1, 12; 8:9, 15, 17; 9:3, 6, 9 (2x), 11, 13; 10:5.

The frame narrator, however, presents a counterbalance to Qohelet's views. In highlighting humanity's whole duty to God as fearing and obeying him (Eccl 12:13), he urges us readers to focus more on our relationship with the Lord and response to his word. That implies that we leave anything frustrating, disappointing, or provoking for him to deal with. He is in control and things happen under his purview even if we do not understand, because we do not have the bigger picture. At the same time, we are fully cognizant that everyone, even those who wronged us, must answer to God (Eccl 3:15, 17; 11:9; 12:14). However someone may respond to our compassionate gestures, we must continue faithful in fulfilling the commandment to love our neighbors as ourselves.

A Tale of Wisdom and Folly

Instead of a parable, Qohelet tells a story of an incident he witnessed that greatly impressed him (Eccl 9:13–18). A powerful army besieged a small city with few inhabitants. Clearly, they did not stand a chance. One of the residents, a poor but wise man, conceived a plan that successfully delivered the city from certain destruction. His wisdom proved the critical factor and impressed Qohelet, who is no slouch himself with regard to wisdom. One immediate lesson we can derive from this story is that it takes a wise person to recognize wisdom. Qohelet alludes to this principle when he writes: "The quiet words of the wise are more to be heeded than the shouts of a ruler of fools" (Eccl 9:17). The adage "the squeaky wheel gets the grease," although less poetic, still proves true. People who loudly complain or cause problems often get more attention than someone who quietly endures and maintains a low profile. This verse explains why the man's wisdom was despised and later ignored and he was soon forgotten (Eccl 9:15c, 16b). He did not boast or flaunt his wisdom and deeds. Likely, he quietly went about saving the city and did not demand that his fellow citizens acknowledge or recompense him in some way. He was not only wise but also humble.

Qohelet twice makes an "x is better than y" comparison: "Wisdom is better than strength" (Eccl 9:16a) and "Wisdom is better than weapons of war" (Eccl 9:18a). The two comparisons say essentially the same thing, as strength and weapons of war are quite compatible. In repeating, Qohelet puts great emphasis on the value and power of wisdom.

Only fools fail to appreciate wisdom. But Qohelet recognizes that folly or foolishness, as undesirable and worthless as it may be, still has a power of its own. Indeed, he admits: "but one sinner destroys much good" (Eccl 9:18b) and "As dead flies give perfume a bad smell, so a little folly outweighs wisdom and honor" (Eccl 10:1). Even a little foolishness can negate what wisdom accomplishes. In that sense, folly is more powerful than wisdom but leads to ruin and much evil.

This lesson on the comparative merits of wisdom and foolishness applies to practicing neighborliness in the marketplace. Both the worker who helps and the one who is helped must exercise wisdom for the dynamic between them to benefit their organization. Drawing a parallel from Qohelet's story, the wise man and the inhabitants of the city correlate with the worker who helps and the worker who is helped, respectively. An important inference we may draw from the tale is that short-term gain—that is, the deliverance of the city—can be obtained in spite of the city inhabitants despising and forgetting their wise deliverer. But long-term gain—permanent benefit—remains remains elusive should folly enter into the picture to ruin any chance of lasting results. For example, another army can besiege the city in the future and, not having learned its lesson or valuing wisdom, it may succumb to the next attack. Identifying with the wise rescuer, we assist a colleague, exercising compassion as well as wisdom in seeking the most effective way to help and also in fulfilling our own responsibilities without penalty. But at the same time, our colleague, too, needs wisdom in maximizing the benefits of our intervention. Have they learned the lesson or acquired the skill we strive to impart? Have they gained sufficient confidence and independence from here on? Or will they need repeated help and remain stuck in their current predicament? Hence, regarding colleagues as neighbors requires another objective or characteristic—the acquisition of professional knowledge and skill.

More Permanent Benefit

Acquiring professional knowledge and skill needs to be the aim of both the worker helping and the one being helped. Lending a helping hand, while noteworthy and certainly to be practiced, represents only a temporary benefit. In treating the wounds of the victim, the Samaritan performed the role of a paramedic and sought the man's healing and recovery. He did not simply bandage the wound but applied medicinal ointment. He was also prepared to sponsor the man's stay at the inn for a significant period of time. Apparently, he did not set limits to the expression of his pity. As neighbors, then, we may consider how to help colleagues acquire the necessary professional knowledge and skill in order to serve them well long-term.

Qohelet presents a short series of proverbs that speak to this aim. He writes: "Whoever digs a pit may fall into it; whoever breaks through a wall may be bitten by a snake. Whoever quarries stones may be injured by them; whoever splits logs may be endangered by them" (Eccl 10:8–9). Simply performing a task is too narrow a focus. Attendant realities and ramifications may accompany the work that greatly affect the end result. What additional considerations need to be factored in so that one can ensure full success? Professional knowledge addresses the proper manner of doing something and stays alert to possible negative consequences that could result from completing the task wrongly or without proper precaution. Each task mentioned in the four proverbs above represents ordinary, everyday work. And each harbors a potential danger if not given adequate preventative caution and care.

Then Qohelet adds: "If the ax is dull and its edge unsharpened, more strength is needed, but skill will bring success" (Eccl 10:10). Here, a combination of right knowledge and skill dramatically improves the chances of securing success in achieving one's objectives. Knowledge recognizes that a sharpened ax will chop much more efficiently than a dull one. Then the skillful handling of the tool will lead to greater success.

Another proverb follows: "If a snake bites before it is charmed, the charmer receives no fee" (Eccl 10:11). No one gets paid for a job partially completed. If the charmer fails to charm the snake, either he lacks the requisite skill or he has not finished his work. This calls for proper work ethics. Does he care enough to perform his duties properly and to exercise precaution in ensuring the safety of his customer?

Being a good neighbor may necessitate our concern in three areas when helping a colleague—professional knowledge, skills, and ethics. The latter area typically lies in the jurisdiction of management, which determines the culture and climate of the workplace. We do not advocate crossing forbidden boundaries. But we can certainly try to do our part in preserving moral principles and practices. We safeguard our own speech, actions, and attitude in the conduct of our business. We should welcome feedback from colleagues or management when we deviate from what is morally proper. Our blind spots may leave us unaware of our transgressions. And as neighbors, we strive to alert our coworkers of perceived moral indiscretion tactfully, privately, and with genuine concern for their welfare.

The Workplace Mentor

Reviewing Ecclesiastes overall, we find that Qohelet has accumulated a significant amount of life and work experience. Endowed with superior wisdom and enjoying the prerogatives of a reigning monarch, he feels compelled to share his observations, findings, and insights to another generation. He wants his readers to understand and accept the reality, sometimes raw and other times mysterious, of life. Holding nothing back, he openly and honestly shares his story, not softening the hard edges but recounting his successes and failures. He also advises, exhorts, and warns, eagerly desiring his readers to take his message and lessons to heart.

We can consider adopting some form of Qohelet's role as teacher and mentor in the workplace, especially if we managed to gain considerable work experience and have a respectable track record of performance. I will address this role from the perspective of a church member who is a marketplace veteran in relation to their fellow marketplace members in a later chapter. But for now, I look at those of us occupying a more senior role in our respective organizations who sense a responsibility toward junior colleagues. This arrangement would be another form of "colleagues as neighbors" in a structured way.

We will address a number of issues in the following order—taking the initiative, personal chemistry, determining the agenda, and the approach. The first issue, taking the initiative, looks at how and when the mentor-mentee relationship begins. Obviously, there must be at least two coworkers who differ in marketplace experience and skill, one further along their career trajectory than the other. Both see the advantage of having such a relationship. But who specifically takes the initiative, the potential mentor or potential mentee? Actually, either can make the first move. Historically, we do not know whether Qohelet initiated writing or responded at the behest of others. The frame narrator declares: "Not only was the Teacher wise, but he also imparted knowledge to the people" (Eccl 12:9a). As king, his building projects were highly visible for all to see and his wisdom likely gained renown. Enjoying all the outward trappings of success, he possessed unquestioned credibility—who would dare challenge the veracity of his teaching?

Conceivably, the junior staff member may take the initiative in asking the senior coworker for advice, counsel, and even a mentoring relationship. They see the obvious benefits in picking their senior colleague's brains. Or the senior coworker sees the other struggling or lacking important knowledge and skills and feels compelled to help accelerate their professional progress. It does not matter who starts the process; the important point is that it begins.

An obvious factor pertains to the personal chemistry and professional relationship between the two coworkers. Are they friendly and get along on a social level? Are they comfortable with each other? Is there openness and honesty between them? Does the junior member respect the other's experience and accomplishments? Professionally, are they on the same team/in the same office office or department? Do they work directly with each other, and if so, is there a supervisory relationship already? All these considerations do not necessarily mean that the mentoring dynamic should automatically proceed or not. Human relationships are complex. But these factors ought to be examined carefully.

Qohelet determined his own agenda without consulting anyone else. Given his unsurpassed wisdom and royal position, with whom could he consult? The frame narrator states: "He pondered and searched out and set in order many proverbs" (Eccl 12:9b). By "set in order," he likely meant Qohelet had a certain sequence in mind and so arranged his wise sayings accordingly. He set forth his thoughts to demonstrate that life and human activity lack meaning. *Hebel* connotes insubstantiality, transience, and foulness, depending on the particular context. Things do not make sense and appear contradictory—that is, absurd.

In exploring the agenda for the mentoring relationship, both coworkers would discuss and inject their own suggestions. The mentor assesses what the mentee needs to progress in his or her career or to do well in the current job. The mentee sees what knowledge and skills seem lacking that the mentor can help rectify. There may be a give-and-take dynamic and perhaps some negotiation to finalize the agenda before proceeding.

The approach—how the interaction will be characterized in actual practice—requires clarification on both sides so as to calibrate expectations. The interaction could be quite informal or somewhat formal, involving some teaching, discussion, and question and answer. The frequency of meeting and other logistical issues would need to be agreed upon. Some kind of covenant, even if informal, would confirm commitment from both parties. It all really depends on each worker's availability, desires, and needs. Some or all of the mentee's needs may be satisfied by the mentor. If the needs are only partially met, the mentor might identify some kind of supplement to cover the deficiency. Or the mentee may know of other resources to pursue.

With Qohelet as our model, we see how forcefully he asserts his advice, exhortations, and warnings. An example of each kind will suffice. He advises his readers thus: "I know that there is nothing better for people than to be happy and to do good while they live" (Eccl 3:12). He leaves no possibility of an alternative to his recommendation to do good. Given his stature as king, teacher, and wise man, his advice takes an imperatival thrust. It would be foolish to dismiss or ignore the advice of a monarch, one of the wisest of men. He exhorts: "Do not be quickly provoked in your spirit, for anger resides in the lap of fools" (Eccl 7:9). Obeying this command-like admonition makes one wise; ignoring it renders one a fool. Exercising forbearance will result in something positive or beneficial; failing to do so leads to dire consequences. Then he cautions: "Do not revile the king even in your thoughts, or curse the rich in your bedroom, because a bird in the sky may carry your words, and a bird on the wing may report what you say" (Eccl 10:20). Secret thoughts and spoken words cannot remain hidden, especially if they pertain to powerful and influential people. Powerful people can certainly cause substantial grief and pain if they perceive these thoughts and words as insulting or as a threat.

Similarly, mentoring may involve advising, exhorting, and warning. As a neighbor, the mentor has the mentee's best interest in mind. But unlike Qohelet, the mentor may be able to personally journey with the mentee. Presence can exert a profound influence and leave a lasting impression long after the mentoring relationship ends and the two go their separate ways.

Being a Friendly Neighbor

In the broader sense, apart from helping a colleague or being a mentor, we can strive toward befriending coworkers. Obviously, the workplace is not a social club, and professionalism should mark all relationships. However, we can still promote cordiality and a pleasant working environment where mutual respect and care characterize interactions.

If we turn the concept of *hebel* on its head and reverse it, we have a positive guideline. First, insubstantiality becomes substantiality where we fulfill our professional responsibilities in a manner that meets the expectations of management, team members, and others. We say what we mean and keep our promise if any is given. We prove trustworthy and aboveboard. Who we are professionally will filter into less formal interactions. We maintain our integrity and demonstrate sincerity in all relationships. Even at the social level, we exercise consistency in taking an interest in colleagues, and not just professionally. We may or may not engage socially outside of work hours, but we can still be friendly and concerned for their well-being within the office.

Second, transience becomes long-term engagement. Typically, we interact with coworkers so long as we both work on the same team or in the same department or organization. Once one of us transitions to another part of the company or to a different company altogether, we could lose contact with each other. Then these relationships are transient. However, we can commit to longer-lasting relationships that transcend our relative location of work so that we can potentially pursue deeper involvement with others. This tenacity communicates genuine interest in and care for others.

Third, foulness becomes fairness and wholesomeness. Although we may try to maximize our chances for a raise, recognition, and promotion, we respect and care enough about colleagues that we do not intentionally do anything to undermine their own chances of moving forward. Should a coworker advance beyond us, we do not harbor envy or jealousy, where envy connotes discontentment or covetousness over the other party's good fortune and jealousy refers to a perceived rivalry. Instead, we applaud our coworker and wish them every success. On the other hand, we respond with indignity and concern when a fellow employee suffers injustice. Even though we may not have been involved, we do not remain neutral and uncaring. If a possible recourse exists, we encourage the affected worker to seek restitution. But if not, we can offer whatever support we can, even if it is only emotional support.

Being good neighbors to colleagues really corresponds to being good friends.

CONCLUDING THOUGHTS

Being a good neighbor to a professional colleague can assume various forms. It can be quite formal, as in a mentor-mentee relationship. Or it can look like two colleagues working well together on a project, mutually supporting each other. But even if they do not directly work together on the same team/in the same office or department, they can still develop a friendship or at least be cordial as fellow professionals. Neighborliness requires intentionality—being open to and even pursuing possible relationships that begin with causal conversation, perceived needs to be met, and opportunities to know one another beyond the superficial. Since work hours represent a significant chunk of the workweek, God's commandment to love one's colleagues as neighbors compels us marketplace workers to take his word seriously and to obey. For we know God will judge our motives and deeds and determine "whether [they are] good or evil" (Eccl 12:14).

CHAPTER 4

Pursuit of Balance

People exhibit mixed reactions to the topic of work-life balance. Studies have shown that the concept of balance means different things to different people, especially across generational boundaries.[1] Even within the same generation, people can differ. A relatively new buzzword has replaced "balance": "flexible work environment." The two overlap, but not completely. Usually, work and life represent two separate but complementary components of life, a twofold compartmentalization. "Work" refers exclusively to the time spent in the marketplace. "Life" means everything outside of work, including family and other activities. A flexible work environment, on the other hand, alludes to flexible working hours, a pleasant workplace, an opportunity for telecommuting, and personal time off, whether for vacation or taking care of personal matters—all of which can promote better health physically and emotionally, reduced stress, and greater productivity. Workers express interest in careers and working arrangements that promote and support their lifestyles. But however one may choose to view the topic, whether as balance or as a flexible work environment, one thing is certain: just about everyone considers this very important, an indispensable. Even those who do not care to achieve balance for themselves because of career ambition or being workaholics would not judge others for having this objective.

1. See Kohll, "Work-Life Balance." Kohll identifies the following distinct generations: baby boomers, Gen X, and millennials.

THOUGHTS FROM ECCLESIASTES

If I may make an analogy between the lament in Ecclesiastes over the inability to enjoy the fruit of one's labor (6:2–3, 6) and the desirable goal of finding satisfaction in one's toil (5:18–19), and the stories we have all heard of work intensity and the difficulty of securing satisfactory balance, then I suggest that many have experienced the truths depicted in this wisdom writing. Achieving balance is tantamount to attaining satisfaction. A possible implication emerging from the biblical text is that balance is susceptible to life's vicissitudes. In that case, the ideal of balance represents insubstantiality, one of the nuances of *hebel*—a central motif of Ecclesiastes.

Balance as God's Gift

Qohelet states that God grants the gift of temporary, momentary pleasures of food and drink and labor in Eccl 2:24, where "to eat and drink" is a synecdoche for the totality of one's life. "Balance," then, encompasses life in the here and now—the satisfaction of fulfilling responsibilities in all the major spheres of one's life. Balance is a gift from God. As Qohelet asks rhetorically, "For without him, who can eat or find enjoyment?" (2:25).

In the section where Qohelet bemoans the human inability to discern and implement perfect timing in regard to the normal events and activities of life (3:1–14), he infers some truths. First, God has implanted in the human heart a sense of the eternal, the big picture (3:11b). Yet, they cannot comprehend God's actions (3:11c), implying that what he does constitutes the big picture. Humans cannot see how his actions, spawned by his plans and purposes, affect all that occurs in their lives and in the world, nor can they understand his rationale. They may seek answers, but he is not answerable to them. Second, Qohelet then states: "I know that there is nothing better for people than to be happy and to do good while they live. That each of them may eat and drink, and find satisfaction in all their toil—this is the gift of God" (3:12–13). Qohelet resigns himself to his human limitations. He acknowledges that God is not similarly bounded. In saying that "there is nothing better," he plaintively accepts his fate and that of all people. The best they may hope for is to make the most of this life while they can. Their realistic aspirations are confined to the routine or mundane—eating and drinking and deriving satisfaction from their toil. None of these come close to anything grand or make a significant contribution to the big picture. In contrast, Qohelet declares: "I know that everything God does will endure forever; nothing can be added to it and nothing taken from it. God does it so that people will fear him" (3:14). No human can aspire to God's level; the distance between him and humans is too vast to bridge. Recognizing the gulf invokes deep fear and awe at God and his greatness. No one dares to dream of possibly contributing to God's enterprise. His gift to them is the very limited ability to enjoy this life and find some satisfaction in whatever they manage to do and accomplish. Be content with one's allotment from God and stay within one's boundaries. God's gift reveals his will, and contentment means submission to his will. Thus, seeking and attaining balance is to obey his will, and not achieving it would be tantamount to disobedience.

However, circumstances that lie outside of one's control could pose barriers to balance. In such cases, Qohelet's words ring true: "I have seen another evil under the sun, and it weighs heavily on mankind: God gives some people wealth, possessions and honor, so that they lack nothing their hearts desire, but God does not grant them the ability to enjoy them, and strangers enjoy them instead. This is meaningless, a grievous evil" (6:1–2). Here, *hebel* connotes insubstantiality—what appears promising or substantial disappoints and misleads. People have good jobs and fine families but cannot find satisfaction in them, perhaps because of long work hours and high pressure and precious little time at home.

Qohelet repeats his message (5:18–20). Since life is short, focus on the present and make the most of it, eating, drinking, and finding satisfaction in toilsome labor. All three represent normal activities—nothing out of the ordinary—but collectively, they symbolize the human existence as God has allotted. God's gift is "the ability to enjoy" their wealth and possessions, which he provides (5:19). Do not bother about the bigger picture, about life; instead, enjoy the moment (5:20). Qohelet does not specify the exact nuances of "labor" (5:18) and "toil" (5:19). But since they seem to encompass much of life, we can generalize this activity as any and all kinds of work a person engages in—marketplace toil, domestic chores and family responsibilities, community service, and personal pursuits. The concept of balance incorporates all of them.

Balance as a Priority of the Young

Qohelet's counsel to the younger generation offers some somber thoughts (11:8—12:7). Metaphorically, he likens the years of youth as light and the later years as darkness typified by trouble, with diminishing ability to see and hear as death draws near. He urges the young to make the most of their youth and enjoy life while they can (11:8a, 9a–b) and, at the same time, to remember their Creator, for in their later years they will experience trouble and not be able to enjoy life (12:1).

In order to heed Qohelet's advice, marketplace workers of whatever age should view balance as the primary means to enjoy life fully and to honor their God. They should derive pleasure in each and every facet of life, whether work, family, church, or other areas, including friends, recreation, and personal pursuits. With a vocation of pursuing the common good, which encompasses loving God and neighbor, they should strive to orient all their involvements and activities toward worship and service to God and the well-being of their colleagues, family members, and the general community. Therein rests their finding satisfaction in all their labor (not only marketplace-related labor but also labor in a broader sense to cover other areas of intentional activity).

But as Qohelet admonishes, time is limited; youth is fleeting. So, redeem the time and take full advantage of one's potential and opportunities at the present time. Don't waste time but act decisively and quickly. He gives this encouragement: "follow the ways of your heart and whatever your eyes see" (11:9c). This advice seems to be an open invitation to do whatever a person desires to do. Yet, Qohelet follows with "but know that for all these things God will bring you into judgment" (11:9d). God may not prevent a person from participating in some enterprise, but a day of accountability will come. Although Qohelet does not specify in any detail God's criteria for evaluation, the general tenor of his writing suggests that a person should be mindful of the appropriateness of any activity in its season (3:1–8) and "do good while they live" (3:12b). The "good" is defined in the following verse: "That each of them may eat and drink, and find satisfaction in all their toil—this is the gift of God (3:13). A gift expresses intention. In giving the gift of being able to find satisfaction in life, God desires us to have a life of fulfillment. Given this context, Eccl 11:9c ("follow the ways of your heart and whatever your eyes see") should be interpreted in the context of fulfillment.

Balance is the key to fulfillment. If a person cannot achieve balance, then they cannot honor Qohelet's exhortation: "So then, banish anxiety from your heart and cast off the troubles of your body, for youth and vigor are meaningless" (11:10). In view of the immediate context, "meaningless" (*hebel*) likely connotes transience here (11:8—12:7). Anxiety and troubles characterize the aged, not the young. So, Qohelet exhorts the young to enjoy life and find satisfaction while they still can, before they get old. But if this generation fails to attain balance, they would have wasted their youth in not experiencing what God wants for them. Now is the time to have balance, not later. Imbalance results in anxiety and trouble. So, for those who are single and willingly give up balance in order to spend extra effort and time to advance their budding careers, they may have misspent their youth. As Qohelet implies, current opportunities to find balance that are not taken now cannot be recaptured later. The time has come, and once passed, it is gone forever.

Balance as a Timing Issue

Balance preserves the perfect timing of every facet of life. Qohelet recites a litany of opposing pairs (e.g., planting and uprooting or searching and giving up) in Eccl 3:2–8 where each event has its proper time, and so too does its opposite. Regarding the list (3:2–8) as representative rather than comprehensive, then we may add another opposing pair, each with the proper timing—work and rest, or work life and the rest of life. According to Qohelet's schema, God alone knows the perfect timing or balance of the two paired elements. Humans, on the other hand, cannot know that perfect balance and so strive to achieve it, perhaps through experimentation or attempting to surmount obstacles. But work and life lie outside our total control, implying that we may never attain perfect balance. The operative principle entails that if the timing is right, then balance prevails. But Qohelet states that humans cannot discern the appropriate time (3:9–11). God alone knows, but humans can, at best, make a conjecture in hopes of getting it right. But getting the timing right 100 percent of the time is beyond human ability. So, some imbalance proves unavoidable.

Two of Qohelet's proverbs are relevant to the topic of balance. First, "the toil of fools wearies them; they do not know the way to town" (10:15). Although several interpretations are possible, in view of the wise injunction to use a sharpened ax for more effective toil a few verses before (10:10), I suggest that the fool works hard but not necessarily smart, thereby expending more energy and time than really necessary. As a consequence, fatigue sets in and they have lost their bearings in going to town, where I take "town" as a metaphor for home, given that the worker has labored in the fields. Fools have tired themselves so much from their work that they may not be able to return home in order to spend quality time with their families. They may return so late that they miss their children's waking hours or lack the energy to help out with raising the family. Second, "through laziness, the rafters sag; because of idle hands, the house leaks" (10:18) addresses meaningful participation at home, including domestic chores. Family and lodging require hands-on involvement. But these essential responsibilities remain unfulfilled, whatever the reason—laziness, insufficient time at home, or fatigue due to overwork at the office. Practically, the family does not really care what the reason may be; they feel neglected and suffer. Attaining balance, then, earmarks a worker as possessing the requisite wisdom.

Imbalance as *Hebel*

Without proper balance, labor becomes rather burdensome and stressful. Qohelet states the realistic goal that "a person can do nothing better than to eat and drink and find satisfaction in their own toil" (2:24a), a principle of carpe diem. If we interpret "own toil" as any and all significant activity in which people engage, then toil includes marketplace work, responsibilities at home and at church, and involvement with the local community—essentially, all the major areas of life. Satisfaction emerges when all areas receive proper attention. Hence balance, if achieved, results in satisfaction. As Qohelet affirms, satisfaction and balance are gifts from God (2:24b–25; 3:13b, 22a). Should management be a "slave driver" that cares only for the profit gained and sees employees as merely "clogs in the machine," then such dire conditions call for God's gracious intervention to bestow the gift of satisfaction and balance.

Qohelet follows his observation of injustices in the world with advice to find satisfaction in one's work. He writes:

> There is something else meaningless that occurs on earth: the righteous who get what the wicked deserve, the wicked who get what the righteous deserve. This too, I say, is meaningless. So I commend the enjoyment of life, because there is nothing better for a person under the sun than to eat and drink and be glad. Then joy will accompany them in their toil all the days of the life God has given them under the sun. (8:14–15)

Qohelet seems to imply that, since some injustices have no ready resolution, the best option available would be the practice of carpe diem. In the passage above, "meaningless" connotes the *hebel* nuance of foulness. Because Qohelet does not specify the particular incident of injustice, his generalization invites us to include work-related injustice, such as overly demanding or unscrupulous management or a toxic work environment. Yet, Qohelet urges workers to enjoy life and be glad. There is an apparent incongruity—how can anyone enjoy life in their toil when injustice afflicts them? He seems to suggest that since no available remedy to the injustice presents itself, then make the most of life and enjoy it as much as possible. This advice suggests further that in spite of any injustice suffered, one should still strive for enjoyment and satisfaction. The two terms ("enjoyment" and "satisfaction") are treated interchangeably in Eccl 2:24–25. In the present discussion on balance, then, following Qohelet's urging, we should not allow workplace injustice or difficulty prevent us from pursuing balance and hence satisfaction.

Some workers may experience what Qohelet lamented, beginning with a rhetorical question: "What do people get for all the toil and anxious striving with which they labor under the sun?" (2:22). The implied answer, sadly, is "nothing but grief," as he confirms: "All their days their work is grief and pain; even at night their minds do not rest. This too is meaningless" (2:23). These workers feel tension and unease thinking about their projects in the evenings and on weekends. Try as they might to separate work from the rest of their lives, work-related thoughts and concerns encroach into their consciousness and, as a consequence, their anxiety levels elevate. Their families are affected too. Their troubling work-related thoughts intrude into other areas of life, thereby rocking their enjoyment of their balance. Hence, "meaningless" connotes the *hebel* nuance of insubstantiality—achieving "balance" but not really enjoying it.

But is this situation really balance? I place the term in quotes above to pose the possibility that one may attain all the trappings of balance—sharply delineated work hours, time at home, and engagement with other pursuits of interest—but still not enjoy balance. The idea of satisfaction, or enjoyment, is a theme threaded throughout Ecclesiastes.[2] If people do not find satisfaction or enjoy their lives, then, according to Qohelet, they have not obtained balance. Workers may be physically present with their family, but mentally and emotionally, they are preoccupied with their work—a project behind schedule or overrunning the budget, a demanding boss, difficult colleagues, a toxic work environment. Try as they might to focus on things outside of work in their nonworking hours, work-related thoughts and concerns, anxiety, and tension creep in.

Such a life finds a parallel with Qohelet's words: "What do people get for all the toil and anxious striving with which they labor

---

2. Eccl 2:24–25; 3:13, 22; 4:8; 5:18–19; 6:2(2x)–3, 6; 8:15(3x); 9:9; 11:8.

under the sun? All their days their work is grief and pain; even at night their minds do not rest. This too is meaningless" (2:22–23). The textual context for these gloomy statements concerns the brevity of life and the necessity of leaving the results of one's labor to a successor, whether wise or foolish (2:14–21). Qohelet's primary grief is that he cannot enjoy his profits long-term because his limited life span prevents him from keeping them. His restless nights thinking about these things mirrors workers leading imbalanced lives, afflicted by restlessness and anxiety at night. Such a lifestyle is unhealthy and devoid of joy. Time seems to pass in a blur. Imbalance can take a toll on family. Marriages suffer the strain; children grow up with preciously few memories of good times together with working parents. The prime of life morphs into middle age, and that morphs into old age. Opportunities missed are irretrievable because life is so short. This realization plagues the aged with regret.

Balance covers the physical, mental, emotional, and even spiritual realms. Should any of these areas exhibit some dysfunction, then we can legitimately question whether a person has achieved balance. Balance signifies a healthy, wholesome lifestyle, something God desires for his people. As wise stewards of what God provides, we honor him by aligning with what he desires for us and pursuing that healthy lifestyle. Balance, then, is what Qohelet calls "good" (3:12–13; 5:18). There is a possible moral aspect to the "good," especially as found in Eccl 9:2 and 12:14, implying that God will hold us accountable for the balance in our lives or the lack thereof.

Qohelet, however, portrays a worst-case scenario. Not every worker experiences what he describes. Some do, but not all. Even for those who bring work home mentally if not literally, the stress they may face is not a constant, unrelenting reality but only an occasional or temporary situation. They can still enjoy some of the fruits of their labor. Yet, a few, having very task-oriented managers who show little concern for the staff's well-being, suffer to the degree Qohelet describes. But should they change organizations or their contract expire, their situation will change potentially for the better.

Even if we cannot achieve balance for whatever the reason, do we value it, seek it, and feel disappointment when we cannot have it? Or are we like some people who do not care or who fail to appreciate it? Our attitude matters. The inner person matters to God. We infer this truth from the various allusions in Ecclesiastes to the heart or thoughts of a person. The heart delights (2:8), rejoices/is joyful (2:10; 5:20; 9:7; 11:9a–b), despairs (2:20), ponders a matter (7:2), can be corrupted (7:7), thinks and remembers (7:22), can be ensnared (7:26), conspires evil 8:11; 9:3), harbors wisdom or foolishness (10:2), makes decisions (11:9c), and feels sorrow (11:10). A person has inner thoughts (2:12; 10:20). But the most compelling evidence for the inner life comes at the very end when the frame narrator declares: "For God will bring every deed into judgment, including every hidden thing, whether it is good or evil" (12:14). The reference to "hidden thing" points to the heart and inner thoughts, the motives and inclination. God judges the heart and thoughts and not only outward deeds. Thus, our attitude toward balance matters to God, who places a high premium on our hearts and thoughts. Do we value balance as God does and strive to the best of our ability to attain it? Whether we actually enjoy balance or not may not always be within our ability when faced with circumstances beyond our control. In such cases, I believe God will not hold us responsible.

Before we fault Qohelet for being an extremist with his repeated mantra that meaninglessness pervades all of life, however, we should note that a good portion of Ecclesiastes is autobiographical, especially when the first-person singular pronoun "I" or "my" appears.[3] He writes based on personal experience and observation. Being wise, his insights are valid, and the frame narrator confirms that (12:9–10). Life can be as grievous and marked by *hebel* as he contends. However, the frame narrator provides a counterbalance in highlighting a higher duty than merely pursuing personal or worldly goals: the duty to God (12:13–14). Even with the proper focus on honoring and serving God and pursuing a relationship with him, work and life can still be challenging and burdensome. Scripture does not guarantee that we will not suffer *hebel* in all its various connotations. Other passages label such difficulties and suffering as trials—God testing the believer (1 Cor 3:13; Heb 11:17;

---

3. Eccl 1:12–14, 16–17; 2:1–15, 17–20; 3:10, 12, 14, 16–18, 22; 4:1–2, 4, 7; 5:18; 6:1; 7:23, 25–29; 8:2, 9, 12, 14–17; 9:1, 11, 13, 16; 10:5, 7.

Jas 1:2-3, 12; 1 Pet 4:12). Such tests have as their intended purpose the deepening of faith through obedience to the Lord. And as Eccl 2:24-25 and 3:13 imply, finding satisfaction when one attains balance is God's will, and he grants the ability to do so as a gift.

However, Qohelet does not interpret the afflictions from work and in life in this manner. At most, he states that God makes humanity see how beast-like they are in that both they and the beasts face the same fate: death (Eccl 3:18-20)—very disheartening and not edifying at all. And so, "everything is meaningless" (3:19f)—*hebel* in the sense of transience—because life is short. Then we can permit Ecclesiastes to comment on the various issues pertinent to work and life that make balance very difficult to attain so that we can be prepared mentally and emotionally and not be shocked or mystified, asking why life proves so rough and taxing. At the same time, we should confer with those portions of Scripture that identify such affliction as divine testing with the noble intent that we grow and deepen from the ordeal.

This approach to reading Ecclesiastes with companion scriptural passages from elsewhere reflects the final form of Ecclesiastes. The book begins and ends with a frame that encloses Qohelet's words: Eccl 1:1 and 12:9-14. Two voices, those of Qohelet and the frame narrator, emerge from reading the book. Both voices need to be heard in order for the reader to make the proper interpretation. Thus, as an extension to the two-voice arrangement, reading Ecclesiastes in tandem with other scriptural passages provides the means to insure the appropriate interpretation and application of this valuable piece of wisdom literature.

Balance Requires Wisdom

Wisdom may not prolong one's life over that of the fool (2:14b-21), alter one's fate to differ from that of beasts (3:18-20), or deliver one from the evil times that befall everyone, no matter whom (9:11-12). Even a little foolishness can neutralize the potential good brought about by wisdom (9:16-18; 10:1). Yet, Qohelet espouses wisdom as a superior virtue (2:13-14a; 9:16a, 17a, 18a). His advocacy carries much weight because he is "the Teacher" and king (1:12), unsurpassed in wisdom (1:16a) and having substantial experience exercising it (1:16b).

In view of the brevity of life (2:14-23), he unequivocally proclaims: "A person can do nothing better than to eat and drink and find satisfaction in their own toil. This too, I see, is from the hand of God, for without him, who can eat or find enjoyment?" (2:24-25). He advises his readers to take full advantage of whatever opportunities come along in a short life. Once missed, they are gone and cannot be retrieved. This is the best one can hope for. But these opportunities relate to the common things—the day-to-day things that are not out of the ordinary or unique. Eating and drinking speak of what one needs to live. Toil, too, is an integral and necessary part of life, nothing grand or spectacular. Live fully in the present. Satisfaction connotes balance wherein one leads an ordinary life and pursues their toil, completing all responsibilities across all the areas of life well, not just in the workplace. Coming "from the hand of God," balance represents God's will and desire for humanity. But that requires wisdom, as Qohelet next states: "To the person who pleases him, God gives wisdom, knowledge and happiness, but to the sinner he gives the task of gathering and storing up wealth to hand it over to the one who pleases God. This too is meaningless, a chasing after the wind" (2:26). In view of the fact that those possessing wisdom, knowledge, and skill cannot prevent the possibility of some unworthy person inheriting all they have toiled for (2:21), Qohelet laments that this injustice is meaningless—*hebel* in the sense foulness—and a great misfortune. The same lamentation surfaces at the end of Eccl 2:26, where *hebel* possibly signifies insubstantiality, at least for the sinner.

The two verses do not contradict each other, as they address two different kinds of people. Ecclesiastes 2:21 looks at the person who is wise, knowledgeable, and skillful, and who leaves the fruit of their labor to someone else, as distressful as that may be to Qohelet. But Eccl 2:26 views the sinner who leaves their accumulated wealth to someone who pleases God. Also, the orientation differs: Eccl 2:21 looks to the future—to the successor—but Eccl 2:24-26 focuses on the present. With the wisdom, knowledge, and skill God gives, the person who pleases God can enjoy their food and drink and find satisfaction in their toil. All of these things collectively represent balance. The person who pleases God and is endowed with wisdom, knowledge, and skill can achieve a satisfying life and balance.

Yet, even wisdom does not guarantee balance, as this virtue has its limitations. The wise, for example, cannot ensure balance (2:25) or fathom all that God does (8:17). In order to maximize the chances for securing balance, one must consider the God factor discussed at the very beginning of this chapter. It is a matter of faith in and dependence on him.

CHAPTER 5

Marketplace Incongruities

Expectations and, on occasion, the accompanying disappointment or puzzlement mark our lives. What we anticipate or hope for may stem from planning, projection, or previous experience. Something as commonplace as working hours can surprise us if, for example, our boss makes a demand just before closing that requires us to stay longer. Certainly we would be surprised and perhaps somewhat irritated if we already had plans for that evening. Yet, even if our evenings are open, we do not like having to stay at work. But more significantly, challenging events can occur which we do not or cannot prepare for, do not fully understand, or struggle to accept, thereby presenting a serious dent to the uniformity of life and work—reorganization of the department or even of the company resulting in role reassignment or in retrenchment, new management that introduces a radical shift in the organization's direction or a change in corporate culture, a project not staying within budget or schedule, the loss of a big contract on which one's employment depends, the hoped-for raise or promotion failing to materialize and finding management's explanation unsatisfactory, "dirty" office politics, suspicious management practices, and so on. In the non-corporate world, situations also arise that make life difficult or difficult to understand and accept—abusive parents and the resultant trauma that continues to haunt in adulthood, an investment that swallows one's life savings, a trust betrayed, or—in our current time—the global pandemic of COVID-19 that has ravaged countries and left innumerable families bereaved.

The incongruities of the marketplace in particular and life more broadly speaking prompt a number of questions. What is going on? Is there an explanation? Why is this happening and why me? What did I do to deserve this? Can I do something about it? Christians might ask how God can let this happen to them. Implicitly, they may question God's love and goodness. We have heard these and similar questions, or we may have voiced them ourselves. Things do not make sense; we cannot comprehend circumstances. Life, it seems, is counterintuitive or contradicts our philosophy of life and work. We are mystified, confused, and, if things prove threatening, alarmed and afraid.

Job experienced an incongruity. A righteous man, he could not explain the loss of property and family and eventually his health. His worldview centered on retributive justice—if I lead the right kind of life morally, I should be blessed, but if I do the wrong thing, I can expect dire consequences. But his experience seemed to contradict this principle. So, naturally, he asked what went wrong. Even though he initially agreed when his friends accused him, soon he shifted the blame from himself to God. An injustice had been perpetrated against him, and he sought to exonerate himself in God's law court. In the end, however, God exonerated him in a way (Job 42:7–8) and accepted his intercession for his friends (Job 42:9). Job, however, never understood the real reason why he suffered. But he learned an important lesson—God alone is God, not answerable to anyone, and Job is a mere human being subject to God's authority. As a result, Job repented as he acknowledged the limitations of his ability to understand. He willingly accepted living in tension, where not everything is transparent and easily resolvable, and where contradiction may characterize life. Whether Job himself finally rejected the governing concept of retributive justice remains unclear, but we readers have the opening frame of chapters 1 and 2 of the book and so realize that sometimes things do not make sense, because we do not always have the big picture or a handle on God's rationale.

Marketplace Incongruities

THOUGHTS FROM ECCLESIASTES

The incongruity that Job faced is framed between his blessed condition before (Job 1:2-3) and after his affliction (Job 42:10-17), thus softening his temporary hardship, although we do not know the duration of his suffering. Of course, he did not know his condition was temporary or that his latter blessedness would essentially double. Yet, in the overall scheme of things, this incongruity could almost be viewed as a blip—howbeit a massive one—on Job's radar. And the readers of the book understand the reason behind his suffering, thereby expanding our understanding of God's sovereignty and of how life in all its complexity cannot be reduced to the principle of retributive justice. Sometimes the principle operates as expected and sometimes it does not.

But when we read Ecclesiastes, we do not find any behind-the-scenes explanation or bigger picture, as in Job. Since we readers of Job are privy to this information, we can safely assume the writer knew. But when we turn to Qohelet and the frame narrator, we do not find explicit assurance that they knew. Hence, any incongruity encountered mystifies and potentially confuses, especially when God does not appear in a whirlwind or provides even a quieter response to our inquiries and prayers.

Qohelet's Limited Point of View

Qohelet's motif "under the sun" appears frequently (passages cited in a previous chapter), informing us that his purview focused on this life's experiences and observations in the world. Since he is limited by his physical senses, we suspect he does not have full access to the bigger picture or to God's point of view. That, however, does not imply that he holds a low view of God or discerns no evidence of God's involvement in the affairs of humanity. As I note elsewhere, Qohelet reveres the Lord. Yet, he remains as clueless as Job about things that defy explanation.

Significantly, Qohelet highlights the contrast between the divine and the human. God determines who finds satisfaction and enjoyment from their toil and who does not (Eccl 2:24-26). The important factor is whether a person pleases him or not. Mention of the sinner being shut out indicates the strong moral aspect of the criterion. God lays the burden on the human race (3:10), an allusion to the imposed responsibility of doing everything according to the proper time, in view of the context (3:1–11). Humans sense the existence of the bigger picture that transcends the temporary and things pertaining to this world but cannot comprehend God's activities (3:11). Hence, they should content themselves with finding satisfaction in the here and now—carpe diem (3:12–13). Living within their worldly limitations means living in constant tension, accepting the unexplained or unexplainable as a part of life. Apparent incongruities from the human perspective can surface that, in the larger scheme of things, do not pose a contradiction to God.

In contrast to humans, God's work endures forever and no one can contribute to or deduct from his plans and work (3:14). They may not understand his rationale or the nature of his work. Job represents all of us; God tested him to confirm his righteousness and, at the same time, taught him an invaluable lesson—God's ways can be unpredictable, for he is not bounded by our expectations of him, nor is he answerable. This latter fact can leave us, as it did to Job, in the dark. Our response ought to be repentance if we have harbored an inadequate view of God. Should he deem it necessary, he will exercise his prerogative and withhold information that can potentially clarify any incongruity. Indeed, appreciating this lofty truth about God deepens one's reverence for him. There may also be fear and trembling in knowing that no one can align perfectly with his timing (3:1–11). God's judgment of the human race serves to create a strong sense of distance between the divine and the human (3:17a), and there is a clear reference to the basis of judgment resting squarely on the appropriate timing of every activity (3:17b).

He confronts humans with the realization of their shared fate with animals—death (3:18–20). A number of times, Qohelet laments the insurmountable barrier of a limited life span. And so, he declares, "Everything is meaningless" (3:19f), where *hebel* signifies transience. The implication drawn is that, by contrast, God alone is eternal. Adding to the strong sense of transience is the realization that the wise person, although superior to the fool, cannot forestall the time of his or her death any more than the one who lacks wisdom (2:14–21). This truth causes restlessness (2:23). The riddle of life and inevitable death lies outside human wisdom to solve. Here is a glaring incongruity—what value does wisdom offer if it cannot lengthen one's life or ensure that the successor to one's fruit proves worthy? A fool would fare no worse.

The Distance between God and Humans

Then Qohelet counsels worshipers regarding the proper attitude and etiquette when entering the house of God (5:1–7). He makes the significant statement that "God is in heaven and you are on earth, so let your words be few" (5:2b). The relative positions of God and humanity connote divine exaltation and honor in contrast to humility and lowliness. The vast distance between the two locations is unbridgeable. Yet, one can approach God in terms of communication—worshipers listen, minimizing extraneous words spoken, which implies they should seek God's voice. The relationship is characterized by fear (5:7b). In view of the danger of angering God, who in wrath will destroy one's works, the fear seems to connote dread—trembling. This recalls the Mount Sinai experience when God descended to the top of the mountain with thunder, lightning, a trumpet blast, and billowing thick smoke like that of a furnace (Exod 19:16–18; 20:18–21). The people carefully maintained a respectful distance lest they die from coming too close. Only Moses could approach and go up the mountain at the Lord's invitation. Indeed, the people requested that Moses mediate between God and them rather than risking having God speak to them directly and then perishing. Such fear, trembling, and distance in the Mount Sinai event also mark entering the house of God. But Qohelet offers no mediator and no outward signs of God's awesome presence appearing. However, the consequences of any disrespectful failure to keep the distance remain very real, as Qohelet warns. According to Qohelet, maintaining distance is accomplished by abstaining from vows and excessive speech—that is, getting overly familiar and nonchalant with God—and by maintaining silence before God.

This cautious approach seems to imply that the worshiper ought not to presume on God by demanding answers about the incongruities of life. The restriction, however, applies only to ill-conceived vows, not to inquiries. So, one can ask but has no promise of clarification.

Incongruity in Qohelet's Writings

Facing life's apparent contradictions is one thing, but finding incongruities in Qohelet's own writings and musings can prove disturbing. Does he contradict himself? And if he does, can we trust his wisdom enough to accept his counsel and admonitions?

Questionable Superiority of Wisdom over Folly

An example of incongruity relates to the value of wisdom compared to that of foolishness. Qohelet praises the superiority of wisdom when he states: "I saw that wisdom is better than folly, just as light is better than darkness. The wise have eyes in their heads, while the fool walks in the darkness" (2:13–14a). The metaphor of light and darkness serves to contrast wisdom and folly. The sharpness of the contrast permits no shades of gray—either a person is wise or a fool, with no states in between. The wise see clearly the path and direction they should take, but the fool gropes blindly and helplessly. Then immediately Qohelet offers a devastating caveat:

> But I came to realize that the same fate overtakes them both. Then I said to myself, "The fate of the fool will overtake me also. What then do I gain by being wise?" I said to myself, "This too is meaningless." For the wise, like the fool, will not be long remembered; the days have already come when both have been forgotten. Like the fool, the wise too must die. (2:14b–16)

Qohelet's lament focuses on either the inevitability of death, which no amount of wisdom can prevent, or on the limitations of life, which wisdom cannot lengthen. Here, he bemoans the limitations of human wisdom—its inadequacy to affect certain fundamental aspects of life. One immediate counter-thought, however, emerges—what about the quality of life, which one's wisdom or folly can impact? Does that not count for something? Qohelet, it appears, feels overwhelmed with the inevitable. With his unparalleled wisdom, he achieves great success and receives rewards commensurate with his achievements (2:4–10). His initial delight, however, changes to gloom when he reevaluates all his work and concludes that it all amounts to nothing—that it is totally "meaningless, a chasing after the wind; nothing was gained under the sun" (2:11c–d). The overall context suggests that Qohelet uses the term "meaningless" (*hebel*) in two possible senses—transience and insubstantiality. His expression "a chasing after the wind; nothing was gained under the sun" indicates insubstantiality, since all the effort amounts to nothing—futility.

Yet, we wonder if this lament is well-founded. Given the finite life span of humans, Qohelet seems to buck against the impossible. He aspires to exceed human boundaries, indicating a different sort of incongruity—a mere man desiring to become godlike (cf. 3:14, where God's work lasting forever indicates that God himself is eternal). We suspect that Qohelet is frustrated and disappointed, feeling confined because his ambition exceeds his abilities. Should he not content himself with being human and already having far more than any other human, given his wisdom and seemingly limitless resources?

This pining for something more—something out of reach—implies another incongruity that contradicts Qohelet's admonition to find satisfaction in all one's toil (2:24–25; 3:12–13, 22). Satisfaction results from appreciating God's gift of carpe diem. Qohelet does not accept his own advice. He exhorts others to find satisfaction and enjoyment in their toil as their God-given lot in life. But he refuses to heed his own counsel. In this regard, is he not incongruent and contradictory? Or does he see himself as being far superior to other humans? His unbridled ambition and dreams would put him on a collision course with God, who gives the gift of satisfaction. Rejecting that satisfaction would be rejecting God's gift. Rejecting God's imposed limits on humanity would be an incongruity.

Inconsistency in Finding Satisfaction from Work

Incongruity surfaces in one of Qohelet's major tenets—carpe diem. His straightforward statement that pleasing God is an infallible criterion to enjoying satisfaction in partaking of daily sustenance and toil (2:24–26) meets an opposing statement when Qohelet laments the evil of when people accumulate wealth, possessions, and honor but God, for some unexplained reason, prevents them from enjoying these things (6:1–2), or the person fails to enjoy their prosperity, regardless of how long they live (6:3–6). The only way to reconcile the conflicting statements, it seems, is to assume that failure implies displeasing God in some way, even though that reason is not brought out explicitly. Just as disturbing, Qohelet plaintively declares that no one ever finds satisfaction from their toil (6:7).

In the carpe diem passages (2:24; 3:13; 5:18; 8:15; 9:9), the term "toil/labor" may signify the actual work performed or the fruits of the work, but the term's usage favors the second meaning: the fruit or pleasure derived from such toil.[1] Pleasure or enjoyment results only if the compensation for the labor proves adequate. Qohelet does not specify what wage amount is sufficient. What amount meets expectations and constitutes a fair recognition of the labor completed? Who or what determines the amount to be received? The principle of carpe diem stands, but in a given situation the laborer may or may not experience satisfaction. Then a potential incongruency may occur.

Divine Justice Enforced or Not

Another incongruity rests in the tension between passages affirming divine justice and other passages that tend to call into question God's juridical intervention. Qohelet observes the evil in the world that defies justice (3:16) but affirms God as the great equalizer: "I said to myself, 'God will bring into judgment both the righteous and the wicked, for there will be a time for every activity, a time to judge every deed'" (3:17). This latter statement forms an inclusio

---

1. Fox, *Qohelet and His Contradictions*, 55–57.

with the earlier "there is a time for everything, and a season for every activity under the heavens (3:1). Thus, the section 3:1–17 forms a literary unit by which one may interpret Qohelet's statement on divine justice. God determines the appropriate time for everything (3:11a), and that includes the appropriate time for judging the deeds of humanity. This truth implies the possibility that wicked deeds may continue for a while until the time of judgment and accountability arrives. People may suffer affliction by the wicked, and the wicked may continue unopposed. No immediate relief or justice may occur. Understanding the operating principle of divine timing can alleviate the puzzlement about God's justice in a world characterized by injustice. Apparently, he does not always respond in judgment immediately in calling into account every wrong or evil perpetrated unless this accords with his timing. But that principle leads to a possible incongruity. Qohelet acknowledges that "no one can fathom what God has done from beginning to end" (3:11c). Humans do not know God's timing on anything, including his exercising judgment and implementing justice. Indeed, humans suffering under the hands of the wicked want immediate relief and deliverance, but if these desires do not accord with God's timing, deliverance does not happen and they continue to suffer. They may complain to God, but he does not respond because it is not the time. They may interpret his inactivity as unjust and may be tempted to accuse him of being unrighteous or unable to deal with the wicked. Their fallacious interpretation is a human incongruity.

Another pertinent passage is 8:2–17, which addresses the issue of justice when God's active role in the affairs of humanity seems to fade in and out. Verses 2–6 admonish one to submit to the king's authority to keep one's oath made before God to do so. Implicit is the thought of accountability to God with respect to one's relationship with the king. Shortly later, Qohelet notes the entrapment of the wicked in their wickedness (8:8d). Since he identifies wickedness, not God, as what enslaves the wicked, we are left to ponder whether Qohelet alludes to the natural consequences of evil deeds (whereby the wicked sink ever deeper into the mire of evil apart from God's active involvement), or to God operating behind the scenes. In the very next verse (8:9b), the self-harm a person inflicts for lording over others likewise appears to be a natural consequence of evil.

The statement that the wicked are buried after a life of avoiding the consequences of their evil ways and of even enjoying honor before others (8:10) leads to Qohelet's concluding epitaph—"this too is meaningless" (8:10c)—where the nuance of *hebel* is foulness. This interpretation is substantiated by the following verse: "When the sentence for a crime is not quickly carried out, people's hearts are filled with schemes to do wrong" (8:11). Although these two verses (8:10–11) appear to contradict the adage of natural consequences for evil (8:8d, 9b), Qohelet immediately brings the matter to a head: "Although a wicked person who commits a hundred crimes may live a long time, I know that it will go better with those who fear God, who are reverent before him. Yet, because the wicked do not fear God, it will not go well with them, and their days will not lengthen like a shadow" (8:12–13). Now Qohelet brings God into the human experience. People's personal fate depends on their attitude toward God—reverence toward God accrues benefits, whereas a lack of reverence toward God leads to negative consequences. However, since Qohelet does not specify the nature of the benefits and consequences, we do not have a sense of the magnitude of the difference, thereby potentially weakening the motivation to fear God. Yet, even within these latter verses, an incongruence occurs with the concluding declaration, "their days will not lengthen like a shadow," when we contrast the possibility that the wicked may live a long time and have ample opportunity to multiply their crimes.

Next, Qohelet laments one of the most glaring incongruities in life: "the righteous who get what the wicked deserve, and the wicked who get what the righteous deserve" (8:14b). This lament is sandwiched between his double pronouncement that this injustice is meaningless (8:14a, c), where *hebel* connotes foulness. Ironically, Qohelet himself seems to be incongruent in stating both that God holds everyone accountable (8:12–13) and that people do not receive what they deserve (8:14). But his critical proviso—"that occurs on earth" (8:14a)—reduces the incongruity. True, the wicked may get away with their evil deeds in this world, but that leaves open the possibility of a divine reckoning that awaits them at another point in time. Hints of inevitable judgment emerge in 3:16–17: "And I saw something else under the sun: In the place of judgment—wickedness was there, in the place of justice—wickedness was there. I said to myself, 'God will bring into judgment both the righteous and the wicked, for there will be a time for every activity, a time to judge every deed.'" In line with Qohelet's pairing of opposing events (3:2–8), where each occurs in its appropriate time and season (3:1), we might insert another pair of events: a time to judge and a time to withhold judgement. Each event has its corresponding opposite. God alone determines when every human deed comes under his review and judgment (cf. 3:11, 14). Ultimately, no one gets away with anything. But this thought assumes God's verdict will be appropriate to the deed. Yet, we ask, who decides what is appropriate? As one scholar has observed:

> Qohelet assumes that God judges but only according to his own standard. In other words, Qohelet merely states that God will judge the righteous and wicked but he does not provide the verdict. He keeps this open. Perhaps an ostensibly wicked person might not receive the severe punishment expected by most Jews. Or perhaps the righteous person might be found guilty.... This strategy preserves God's sovereignty yet allows Qohelet to be honest about the many injustices in life. Qohelet is saying that the fates of humans seem fickle, but God will judge as he sees fit. It is not for mortals to question God's judgment.[2]

The Issue of Theodicy from Qohelet's Perspective

Qohelet portrays God as sovereign. Yet, he appears to limit his authority when, as Creator, he makes humanity upright and they go astray (7:29), implying a measure of freedom for them to follow their inclinations. Here must be an incongruity that disappoints God—he meant for people to fear him and be righteous, but they instead do not fear him and live without regard for his intentions. Hence, Qohelet depicts humanity as incongruous, failing to honor

---

2. Sneed, *Politics of Pessimism*, 185.

their Creator. This characteristic can explain, at least to a certain degree, the incongruities in life. We need to accept the blame for some of the messiness in our lives. There is also an element of unpredictability in that God's response to human decisions and actions does not always align with their expectations.[3] Justice does not always prevail (8:14). Is this, then, another instance of incongruity where human expectations of what God will do does not appear to match his actions?

The tension between God's sovereignty and goodness and the existence of injustice in the world and human suffering—expressed more mildly as incongruities—transitions quickly to the topic of theodicy, where one strives to find the acceptable balance between these truths or assumptions.[4] A reading of Qohelet affirms his high regard for God as sovereign, just, and benevolent. The gift of carpe diem (2:24–25; 3:12–13, 22; 5:18–19; 8:15; 9:7–9) represents the one unequivocal benevolent gesture Qohelet repeatedly emphasizes. But he appears to vacillate about God's justice. He is not accusing God of injustice per se, but his perception of injustice in the human experience based on the available evidence and observations "under the sun" seems undeniable. He does not try to defend God but simply recounts what he has seen: sometimes people get what they deserve, and sometimes they do not. He offers no explanation; life is just that way. But he calls such discrepancies *hebel*, or foulness.

After concluding that God and his ways lie cloaked in mystery, beyond comprehension even for the wise (8:16–17), Qohelet reflects further, not letting the matter rest. He acknowledges that God determines the fate of the righteous and wise, but he remains ambivalent about whether love or hate awaits them (9:1). The way he

---

3. Weeks, *Ecclesiastes and Scepticism*, 153.

4. For a brief review of approaches for addressing theodicy, see Sneed, *Pessimism in Ecclesiastes*, 177–90. Meister and Drew cover the five views of theodicy in *God and the Problem of Evil*. The five views are the Classic view (God permits evil and suffering as a part of his redemptive plan), the Molinist view (God knows what creatures will do in all possible scenarios), the Open Theist view (God does not know the future), the Essential Kenosis view (God cannot control creatures and so cannot prevent evil), and the Skeptical Theism view (rejects any attempt at developing a theodicy and posits that one cannot know God's intentions).

couches his statement leaves open the identity of the source of love and hate—is he inferring that God loves or hates, or is he thinking of fellow humans who may show love or hate to the righteous and wise? Regardless of which option seems more likely, their fate could swing between the extremes of love and hate, with the former being obviously preferable. But Qohelet offers no assurance that God will lovingly favor the righteous and wise. His remark seems to indicate that God may be arbitrary in dealing with the righteous and wise. This impression gets reinforced by Qohelet's following comment:

> All share a common destiny—the righteous and the wicked, the good and the bad, the clean and the unclean, those who offer sacrifices and those who do not. As it is with the good, so with the sinful; as it is with those who take oaths, so with those who are afraid to take them. (9:2)

It does not seem to matter whether a person is righteous or wicked, honorable before God or not. All suffer the same fate. Then the obvious implication is that morality does not factor into determining one's destiny. But, to Qohelet's credit, he labels such moral arbitrariness as evil (9:3a). He, at least, has some sense of morals even if God seemingly does not. Unsurprisingly, humanity harbors evil in their hearts, and the resultant madness typifies their lives (9:3c). Qohelet has already described humanity in similar terms earlier in Ecclesiastes (8:11). When God does not intervene sovereignly, people pursue wickedness unabated. The only solution to the problem of human evil that Qohelet offers is death (9:3d). People are prevented from propagating more evil by their finite life spans, as 9:6 seems to state. How and whether God steps in remains a mystery (8:17). Qohelet reiterates his thoughts from 9:2 in 9:11–12—a person's positive attributes (speed, strength, wisdom, wealth, good education) will not prevent them from meeting the same fate as those lacking those qualities. It's a matter of time and chance, as Qohelet observes. Morbidly, he likens humanity to fish and birds caught in cruel nets and traps. He laments that "people are trapped by evil times" (9:12). They cannot escape. Evil befalls them suddenly.

Such is Qohelet's estimation of reality. God may be good, but people live trapped and helpless, seemingly without hope. Qohelet does not urge his readers to seek God for justice or deliverance. Their fate is sealed and unalterable. God maintains his aloofness, seemingly uninterested and uninvolved. Qohelet's answer to the problem of theodicy is that even though God may be capable of doing something about the evil in human hearts and about the evil times, he chooses not to intervene and allows things to go to their logical conclusion. Suffering and injustice continue unabated. Humans are no better than animals; both are trapped and will die.

The Issue of Theodicy from the Frame Narrator's Perspective

When we come to the frame narrator's concluding remarks (12:13–14, which echoes Qohelet's thoughts in 3:15–17), we find a grander picture in which God will bring every deed and person into judgment, even hidden things. He will determine whether the deed is good or evil. A straightforward reading indicates a future judgment of all people's deeds after they have lived their lives. Being omniscient, God knows every deed done in secret or in the open and evaluates the relative merit of all deeds based on his moral criteria. Like Qohelet, the frame narrator does not delve into the consequences that God will mete out. This final judgment does not preclude consequences faced during one's lifetime; but whether the ramifications align with the rightness or wrongness of a deed or character are not so predictable—sometimes the consequences faced in one's lifetime accord with justice (2:26), and other times they do not (4:1; 5:8; 7:15; 8:10–11, 14; 9:1–3). Qohelet hints that God may well be responsible for some of the injustice experienced (6:1–2). But the frame narrator maintains the orthodox position on God's righteous judgment, where everyone receives what they deserve in the end, even if they escape the consequences during their lifetime.

Marketplace Incongruities

Natural Consequences in Life

Then there are the so-called natural consequences that do not necessarily point to moral culpability or to God's direct intervention but are simply the realities of life under the sun (5:9–12; 9:11–12; 10:8–11, 18). For example, a snake handler gets bitten by the snake and, as a result, receives no fee (10:11). The handler could have been careless or distracted, or the snake may have been unusually aggressive. It is the nature of things. Sometimes bad things happen, even if circumstances are essentially the same as in other incidents when things went well. But in view of the prevailing evil of the times, where people tend to be ensnared or entangled (9:12), bad things are more likely to occur than good things. People should expect this and not be surprised when they suffer. This pattern might be an ancient version of the so-called Murphy's Law ("Anything that can go wrong will go wrong"). This reality accords with Qohelet's general viewpoint on life overall. He opens and closes his writings by calling everything utterly meaningless, forming a grand frame, or inclusio (1:2; 12:8), that summarizes his conclusions based on his life experiences and experimentations. Armed with superior wisdom, he exercises keen insight. Unfortunately, his musings lead to frustration, disillusionment, and resignation toward life, along with a sense of dread before a distant God.

Certain consequences clearly result from human error or negligence. A house suffers decay or breaks down due to a lack of regular maintenance on the part of irresponsible owners (10:18). A dull ax potentially signifies a lack of maintenance and, of course, requires more effort to use (10:10). Interestingly, Qohelet does not advise sharpening the tool but to use skill. Does he mean that a skillful person can still use a dull ax effectively? Or would such a person adopt another means of achieving the same ends? If skill is equated with wisdom, a motif of Qohelet's writings, then we might conclude that a wise person would first sharpen the ax before using it.

One sober but natural consequence constitutes the last of Qohelet's musings when he reflects on the encroachment of old age and the inevitability of death (12:1–7). Regardless of one's moral profile, all face the ravages of age. Qohelet characterizes old age as "days of trouble" without pleasure (12:1), darkness (12:2), trembling, a stooped back, fewer friends as one advances in age, dimness (12:3), loss of hearing (12:4), and fear and dampening of desire before death comes (12:5–7). In this way, Qohelet concludes his motif on death (2:14b–16, 18b; 3:2a, 19–21, 22b; 4:2; 5:15–16; 6:3e, 12b; 7:1–2, 4a, 15b, 17c, 26a; 8:8b, 10a; 9:4b, 5–6, 10b). This motif weighs heavily on Qohelet's conscience and serves as the major reason for his overpowering sense of *hebel*—insubstantiality, transience, and foulness.

CONCLUDING THOUGHTS

For Qohelet, perhaps the greatest incongruity is human weakness in the form of a propensity to deviate from God's desire for moral uprightness (7:29; 9:3c), the frustrating limitations of human wisdom (2:15–16; 7:23–24; 8:17), the inability to discern the proper timing of things (3:1–17) or to mitigate the injustice in the world (5:8; 7:15; 8:10–11, 14), the brevity of life (5:18; 6:12)—which is even more difficult because no one has any control over the time of their death (8:8b) and which eliminates any meaningful difference with animals (3:18–20)—and the impenetrability of the mystery cloaking God's activities and intentions (3:11c). Qohelet aspires to greater things. He wants to become like God in his achievements and is frustrated that he cannot, something inferred from his negative statements that nothing can be added or subtracted from God's work (3:14) and that no one can alter what God has done (7:13). In spite of his unsurpassable achievements in completing great projects with the aid of his superior wisdom and nearly inexhaustible resources (2:4–10), Qohelet still laments the meaninglessness of his work (2:11). He finds it all *hebel*, insubstantial. He states his dissatisfaction and disappointment in view of the grand scheme of things (1:3–10). None of his toil has made any fundamental contribution to anything truly new "under the sun," resulting in deep disappointment. And over the course of human history, with its constant procession of generations where each replaces the previous one, he fears that he and his work will soon be forgotten (1:11). Here, *hebel* connotes transience.

Seemingly, the only real positive aspect of life, according to Qohelet, centers on the principle of carpe diem, the here and now. In discussing the "grievous evil" of death, he asks rhetorically, "As everyone comes, so they depart, and what do they gain, since they toil for the wind?" (5:16). He characterizes life as dark, frustrating, afflicted, and filled with anger (5:17). Then he offers the only viable counterbalance: "This is what I have observed to be good: that it is appropriate for a person to eat, to drink, and to find satisfaction in their toilsome labor under the sun during the few days of life God has given them—for this is their lot" (5:18). The only real relief from the depressing reality of an all too brief and insignificant life are the daily pleasures of meals and some satisfaction with one's labor—nothing permanent but instead very momentary.

But when we read the frame narrator and his final words (12:13–14), we uncover an incongruity between him and Qohelet. Rather than dwelling on human weakness and inadequacy, the frame narrator puts the spotlight on God and our responsibility to him. He holds us accountable, and we answer to him. We are fully capable of fearing God and keeping his commandments. Doing good lies within our reach. We can do good and so gain his approval. Then our challenge takes the form of a question: Will we do so?

To be fair, however, Qohelet also acknowledges that God will judge humanity (3:17; 11:9). Yet, we wonder about the basis for judgment as Qohelet understands it. He appears equivocal. He sees God differentiating between those who fear God and those who do not (8:12–13) but immediately bemoans the injustice in the world (8:14). The only recourse offered is carpe diem (8:15)—enjoy life when you can. Essentially, Qohelet gives up because there is nothing that can be done to rectify wrongs, since God will not—so ignore it and embrace whatever joy that accompanies one's toil in life. Qohelet resigns himself to living with the incongruity of a just God who does not uphold justice in the world.

The thoughts and conclusions haunting Qohelet about life's *hebel* nature are not a barrier, according to the frame narrator. He does not totally disagree with Qohelet (12:9–10), admitting that incongruities mark our lives and toil. But he redirects our attention to our responsibility to God. Instead of carpe diem as the final answer, we should be cognizant of our duty to fear God and keep his commandments. The final solution, according to the frame narrator, rests with God bringing "every deed into judgment, including every hidden thing, whether it is good or evil" (12:14). Indeed, God is just and will ratify all wrongs according to his timing (3:17), something about which both writers agree. But the temporal frame of reference may differ—Qohelet seems to locate judgment among all the other events that take place in their appropriate time (3:1–8), whereas for the frame narrator, there is an eschatological nuance. Hence, we can trust that God will address all the incongruities of life, and until then, we strive to fulfill our stewardship.

CHAPTER 6

Role of the Church

Christians in the marketplace are the public face of their faith to their colleagues, who may embrace other faiths. Obviously, the workplace cannot serve as the battleground for theological debate or even overt witnessing. The primary duty of all concerned is fulfilling their KPIs and seeking to help their organization succeed in achieving corporate objectives. Relationships should manifest a professionalism befitting their official roles in the discharge of their responsibilities. Conversations in the office should naturally pertain to the business at hand.

Yet, Scripture calls for disciples to be the salt of the earth and the light of the world (Matt 5:13–14). A fair number of conferences, seminars, books, discussion groups, and other resources address marketplace ministry and witness.[1] So, the intent of the current chapter is not to add to the plethora of resources already available but to ascertain what a reading of Ecclesiastes may contribute to the discussion of the role of the church in relation to the marketplace.

---

1. For example, one resource is *Marketplace Ministry,* the *Lausanne Occasional Paper* 40. This paper features a lengthy bibliography of relevant literature. The Christian Business Men's Connection (CBMC) is a global enterprise facilitating marketplace ministry. BizMin prepares businesspeople through workshops, videos, and courses to do business as ministry. In Asia, there is the Singapore-based Global Business Network (GBN), which strives to bring about transformation in the marketplace.

A FALSE DICHOTOMY

Many marketplace Christians express disappointment with the lack of support provided by churches for their challenges in the marketplace. In fact, they say that their pastors create a dichotomy: work does not count as service to the Lord—only ministering in church does. This compartmentalization makes it nearly impossible for those with long work hours—given the pressures of and time commitment to the corporate world and the difficulty of claiming family time—to devote significant time and energy to the church. To do so would likely demand sacrificing work and family. Something has to give. If the boss and pastor prove unrelenting, that severely marginalizes family time. But how much family time is required to nurture a healthy home? People give different estimations, indicating that a universally accepted amount cannot be attained because each situation differs. For example, marital status, stage in life, work demands, and opportunities to serve in church differ. I don't believe there is a specific amount of time that satisfies everyone. Each person must discern for him- or herself what is adequate.

But even if workers pursue a work-family-church life balance, they still need the understanding and support of their church leaders and the resources to help them deal with work-related issues. Most find the camaraderie of peers in small groups the sole resource within church. But more is needed, they say. How can they persuade their pastors to become more intentional? What if their pastors lack the requisite experience and skills to provide meaningful support? What alternatives exist within their churches and outside?

Moving the church's beliefs and teaching from a dichotomous worldview to embracing the sacredness of all of life—including work, family, and community outside of the church—represents a near herculean task. Is it mission impossible? Perhaps. But we have to keep trying. The two greatest commandments are at stake. In an earlier chapter, I presented professional colleagues as neighbors. Having this viewpoint transforms our attitudes about work relationships with our bosses, fellow team members, other office mates, and clients. Our obedience to those two commandments cannot be restricted to just the confines of the church and its members. Since our Lord superintends all of life, his directives must encompass all of life, including our intentions and activities in the corporate world, in the home front, and in other areas of life. This truth seems clear enough, but the real question in this chapter is whether the church and its leadership acknowledge this in practical and helpful ways that empower its marketplace members to truly function in their work world and in the larger world outside of church.

Reflection from Ecclesiastes

Ecclesiastes offers a parallel to the dichotomy that threatens to compartmentalize life into the sacred and the secular. Qohelet mentions one's duty to God a few times: pleasing God (but he does not explain what constitutes a life pleasing to him) (2:26; 7:26); fearing God (but more in the sense of dread) (3:14); maintaining the posture of a listener in the house of God (5:1–3); keeping one's vows (5:4–7); and remembering one's Creator (12:1)—likely in the sense of coming judgment (11:9). The scarcity of these references serves as a sharply contrasting backdrop for the greater emphasis on making the most of this life: finding daily satisfaction or enjoyment from one's toil (carpe diem) (2:24; 3:13, 22; 5:18, 19c; 8:15); being happy and doing good (3:12, where I interpret "good" as satisfying labor in view of the next verse, 3:13); deriving mutual benefit from human partnerships (4:9–12); enjoying wealth and possessions should God grant the ability to do so (5:19), in contrast to those who cannot enjoy what God has given them (6:1–2); submitting to those in authority to avoid the consequences for not doing so (8:2–5); enjoying life when one can (9:7–9); being blessed to live in a region with effective civil authorities (10:17); diversifying business ventures to reduce the risk of loss (11:1–6); and enjoying one's youthful years before old age and death come (11:7—12:7).

Then Qohelet makes some summary statements encompassing all of life: "They seldom reflect on the days of their life, because God keeps them occupied with gladness of heart" (5:20) and "For who knows what is good for a person in life, during the few and meaningless [i.e., transient] days they pass through like a shadow?

Who can tell them what will happen under the sun after they are gone?" (6:12). Ecclesiastes encloses Qohelet's reflections between a pair of bookends that declare, "'Meaningless! Meaningless!' says the Teacher. 'Everything is meaningless!'" (1:2; 12:8), with the additional "Utterly meaningless!" in Eccl 1:2. "Meaningless," or *hebel*, signifies insubstantiality, transience, and foulness.

Such an overemphasis on life and work in this present world to the relative neglect of one's duty to God demonstrates a skewed view of reality. Qohelet is limited to the physically observable and to whatever his wisdom enables him to perceive about this present life. He harbors a worldview emphasizing carpe diem, the here and now, with some sense of the sacred. But that limited sense makes him acutely aware that God and his activities lie outside the realm of his observations and makes him feel helpless to improve his lot in life, so he counsels his readers accordingly.

The voice of the frame narrator enters in the closing frame (12:9–14) to assess Qohelet and offer a fuller view of reality. The frame narrator approves of what Qohelet observes and laments, but only up to a certain point. The former adjusts the latter's rather myopic grasp of things in order introduce duty to God with greater emphasis. Even if one cannot readily discern God's presence and activity in our lives, faith prompts us to believe that life can be meaningful and even have eternal value if our duty encompasses fearing God and keeping his commandments, the two greatest of which call for a loving relationship with him and with one's neighbors. Qohelet does not seem to understand these relationships, let alone pursue them. Without a meaningful relationship with God, life would degenerate into meaninglessness, resulting in grief, disillusionment, and despair. Hope emerges only from a close walk with God. Thus, the frame narrator points toward a wholistic approach to life and work, one that refuses to compartmentalize, so that all of life is viewed as sacred.

The church can assume the role of the frame narrator in providing a counterbalance to the carpe diem worldview predominant in the main body of Ecclesiastes and in the corporate world in order to facilitate greater awareness of the eternal and of God's presence on the part of its members, especially those in the marketplace. Too often, concern about making a living, pursuing career objectives, family responsibilities, and other interests deemed important can occupy one's full attention in the here and now. As important as this focus may be, it can lead to an overemphasis on oneself—one's needs, desires, and progress toward meeting those concerns—to the point that one may neglect other important considerations, such as the needs of the church, of the community at large, and even of the world. For example, should we harbor an active interest in global climate change and pollution and social injustice in other regions?

But does the church have such a comprehensive vision? If they define Christian stewardship and service as building up the body of Christ—that is, the local church—and responsibility to family, then as noteworthy as these goals may be, this does not encompass responsibility to the marketplace, community, and world. Specifically, what a broader scope entails depends on the church's understanding of God's mandate in the Scriptures. Do they try to correlate the divine promise to Abraham that "all peoples on earth will be blessed through you" (Gen 12:3c) with the commandment "Love your neighbor as yourself" (Lev 19:18b; Matt 22:39)? Do they interpret the blessing both spiritually and materially? True, the "you" in the promise applies personally to Abraham, but it also applies to his descendants after him, with ultimate fulfillment in the person of Jesus Christ. But as a part of the body of Christ, we Christians should assume an active role in being a blessing.

The scope of that blessing finds explicit expression in the second greatest commandment. Loving our neighbor implies blessing them according to our ability. The concept of "neighbor" assumes a far horizon. In his parable, Jesus intentially chose a Samaritan to help the Jew. Jews were members of the covenant community; Samaritans were outside of the covenant. Being a neighbor who loves and blesses transcends covenant boundaries. We bless not only those within the household of God but also those outside. Restricting our responsibility only to members of the covenant community enforces a false dichotomy God never intended. The original scope of blessing "all peoples on earth" signifies a global outreach and concern.

A number of writers observe the passion millennials have for changing the world around them in seeking to make it a better place to live for everyone, not just for themselves.[2] They care deeply about civil rights, racial discrimination, and gender equality, for example, and not only where they live and work—their concerns and involvement extend beyond national borders. They advocate addressing ecological issues affecting the world. But do churches understand this collective characteristic among young people and strive to mobilize the young within its membership, thereby demonstrating relevance? If young people are not convinced that the church cares about what they deem important, why would they continue going to church?

But it is not only about attracting and retaining millennials; it is about staying true to the Scriptures—a wholistic faith that sees all of life as sacred and important to God—hence the necessity of being accountable to him in all areas. Ecclesiastes asserts this view. Qohelet states that "God will bring into judgment both the righteous and the wicked, for there will be a time for every activity, a time to judge every deed" (3:17). The expression "every activity . . . every deed" speaks of the totality of life, not just a portion. All of it comes under divine judgment. Again, "Follow the ways of your heart and whatever your eyes see, but know that for all these things God will bring you into judgment" (11:9c-d). This admonition addresses the young, who have much of their lives before them. Qohelet urges them to live their lives pursuing their dreams, inclinations, and ambition. "All these things" encompasses whatever they intend to do and manage to accomplish throughout their lives. In the end, God will review their deeds and pass judgment. Then, concluding the book, the frame narrator declares, "For God will bring every deed into judgment, including every hidden thing, whether it is good or evil" (12:14). Nothing is excluded from God's purview. Here, both Qohelet and the frame narrator coalesce in total agreement. The criterion of "good or evil" shows that the moral element is the main criterion of the divine assessment. Any and all aspects of life feature a moral dimension, signifying the importance God attaches to it.

---

2. For example, see Economy, "New Study."

According to the divine scheme, a false dichotomy would be evaluated as "evil."

THE YOUNG WORKING GENERATION

Much has been written about millennials in the marketplace.[3] An online opinion piece identifies several factors that millennials find attractive about a particular workplace: a worthy mission to which they can contribute (answering the *why* question); openness to their opinions or views; opportunities to grow professionally and acquire new skills; work flexibility (strong corporate culture, telecommuting, freedom to explore outside interests); philanthropic opportunities; and in-person interaction and authentic relationship building.[4] Companies strive to understand these interests and characteristics with the objective of better leveraging this employee demographic within their organizations in order to achieve their mission objectives more effectively. Will the church follow suit in order to better attract, involve, and support these young people? This generation not only represents the future of the corporate world, but their commitment to the church can ensure its future too.

In order to fulfill its responsibility to these young people, the church, like companies, needs to understand them—their chief characteristics, passions, concerns, and needs. But unlike with companies, the church's interest in them serves to position itself to serve and support them effectively. As companies consider adjustments in their corporate cultures to accommodate this demographic within the workforce, will the church likewise be open to possible changes in its culture and ministry approach? The challenge is

---

3. For example, Petersen discusses the economic struggles of millennials in *Can't Even: How Millennials Became the Burnout Generation*, and Chanos advises millennials on how to survive in the twenty-first century in *Millennial Samurai: A Mindset for the 21st Century*. You can also see "Challenges and Conflicts—Millennials in the Workplace" and Bolden-Barrett's article "Millennials Are HR's Biggest Challenge in the Multi-Gen Workplace," both available online. See bibliography.

4. Little, "6 Ways to Get Along with Millennials at Work." Little is CEO of Eagle Consulting/Counseling Division in various locations in Alabama.

staying relevant and meaningful as society—or, at least, a big part of it—continues to evolve. The gospel stays invariant, but ministering to another generation requires adaptation in order to connect and communicate.

Reflection from Ecclesiastes

In his admonition to the youth, Qohelet states: "Follow the ways of your heart and whatever your eyes see, but know that for all these things God will bring you into judgment" (11:9c–d). Even if they should have many years ahead of them, the young cannot afford to forget the inevitability of divine judgment of their activities and lives. Then Qohelet adds, "remember your Creator in the days of your youth" (12:1a) with a view to the encroachment of old age and death (12:1b–5), followed by a clear allusion to death (12:6–7). The pleasures and possibilities of the youthful years ought not deaden a continued awareness of God, who, as Creator, is the source of life and provides the gifts of satisfaction and enjoyment (2:24–25; 3:13). Moreover, "to the person who pleases him, God gives wisdom, knowledge and happiness" (2:26a).

The church reinforces these important truths through teaching, discipleship, and accountability. But the church can only be effective if the young people continue to faithfully participate in church and submit to its leadership and instruction. If they are delinquent in their attendance or unreceptive to the church's influence, they become more vulnerable to the challenges of life, in accordance with Qohelet's teaching on the advantage of having a companion for the journey ("Two are better than one: . . . if either of them falls down, one can help the other up. . . . A cord of three strands is not quickly broken" [4:9–12]). There is strength and safety in numbers, in being part of the believing community. Only together with members of the church can young people have the necessary collective resources to navigate through life. The possibility of tough times and failure looms, and Qohelet's wisdom about not doing it alone provides the key to not only surviving but even to prospering.

But, at the same time, should they come to church and participate in worship, fellowship, and service, their attitude can determine whether their involvement will prove meaningful and helpful as they pursue their careers and lives. Qohelet admonishes any who venture into the house of God to maintain the proper mindset of a humble, reverent listener eager to hear God's voice (5:1–7). They ought not enter with their own agenda, demanding that he listen to them. He does not do their bidding, but rather they must align themselves to him and seek his will. He is God in heaven above, and they are but humans confined to the world below.

Qohelet perceives the vast gulf between God and himself, although he is exalted as "the Teacher" and king (1:12), blessed with uncommon wisdom superior to all others (1:16), and spectacularly successful in all his grand schemes and enterprises (2:1–10). All his toil, accomplished with wisdom, knowledge, and skill (2:21a), leads to deep disillusionment when he faces the specter of his inevitable death, which will prevent him from enjoying his work long-term and will make him soon forgotten—no different from someone less accomplished and from the fool (2:14–23). In contrast, God and his work endure forever, and no one can oppose him or take credit for his work (3:14). This gulf that Qohelet describes becomes tangible for us when we enter the house of God and sense his holy presence. Scripture consistently portrays God's powerful presence when his people assemble before him in worship and eager anticipation. We stay humble and dare not speak but strive to listen. And when we hear him, the gulf dissipates and we draw near. Should the church facilitate this dynamic, it will have fulfilled its purpose.

THE CHURCH'S MANDATE

As I mentioned earlier, many marketplace members express disappointment with their churches' lack of support in helping them deal with issues at work. A question arises in response: How should the church meet this expressed need, to what extent, and in what form? But perhaps a more fundamental question is this: Should the church challenge its marketplace members to pursue the necessary spiritual maturity and wisdom to apply the church's preaching and teaching in the corporate world for themselves, while the church remains true to its mandate of proclaiming "the message of the cross" (1 Cor 1:18a) and of focusing on "Jesus Christ and him crucified" (1 Cor 2:2)?

But does the matter have to be an either-or proposition? Can it be "both and"? Cannot the church be faithful to the message of Christ while at the same time addressing the marketplace in specific, concrete ways to guide, encourage, and admonish its sheep? Until they attain the spiritual wisdom and discernment to apply biblical principles for themselves, a little "hand holding" can effectively facilitate their spiritual journey. The responsibility of implementation must fall on someone, but who? Does it have to be the pastoral team, or can qualified laity assume leadership in this matter?

Pastors, particularly those who maintain a heavy schedule of preaching, teaching, discipling, and various leadership tasks, cannot devote time and effort to mentoring members in the marketplace. And some pastors have little to no marketplace experience by which to offer concrete advice. But churches have a repository of marketplace wisdom and experience among members who are spiritually mature and industry wise. Can the church mobilize this segment of their congregation to take a leading role by developing an effective ministry strategy, plan, and implementation? Why not?

A number of churches specifically target the marketplace.[5] Some perform periodic "commissioning services" for working members in order to highlight and keep visible their contributions to the kingdom of God. There are industry-specific interest groups, mentor-mentee relationships, marketplace-related seminars and conferences, and sermons that address marketplace issues from a biblical perspective.[6]

---

5. For example, Saddleback Church—with many campuses, particularly in California and also around the world—ministers intentionally to business leaders, many of whom are church members. Mitchell, a one-time member of the pastoral staff and former business leader, offers a glimpse as to how Saddleback supports its marketplace members and others in "Serving Marketplace Leaders."

6. The Colorado Christian Business Alliance, to name one organization, partners with a number of other like-minded organizations to help marketplace Christians integrate faith and work. They conduct conferences and offer valuable resources.

Marketplace-specific parachurch organizations operate not only in the US but also in other regions of the world. For example, some organizations are headquartered in Singapore and represent a much-needed resource to churches and marketplace Christians.[7] Their services are readily available, so even if one's church cannot adequately support one's struggles or issues in the corporate world, there is still hope through networking across churches and Christian professionals elsewhere.

Reflection from Ecclesiastes

Qohelet laments the meaninglessness of life throughout his writings. For example, he acknowledges that wisdom is better than folly (2:13–14a) yet sees no innate advantage, as both the wise and the fool will die and soon be forgotten (2:14b–16); that injustice prevails (3:16); that humans have no advantage over animals, since both, like the wise and the fool, will die (3:18–20); that oppression occurs without relief (4:1; 5:8); and that humanity lacks the ability to benefit from their labor and wealth (6:1–6). All these speak of meaninglessness as insubstantiality, transience, and foulness, three connotations of *hebel*. Most depressing and pessimistic is Qohelet's belief that these observations represent the sum total of human existence. But in the end, the frame narrator appears to respond to Qohelet's musings, acknowledging the general truthfulness of his thoughts but also pointing out that life is more than what Qohelet can comprehend.

This interaction with the frame narrator—something that Qohelet desperately needs but does not seek, perhaps thinking that his wisdom is sufficient—represents what modern-day Christian workers should avail themselves of. If a dialogue could have existed between the two men, they would have found much that they agree on (12:9–10), establishing common ground. Yet, at the same time, the frame narrator points out areas of deficiency (12:13–14), the proverbial blind spots in Qohelet's worldview. Such exchanges exist in church, where believers gather to share, discuss,

---

7. For example, Salt & Light and Global Business Network, to name two.

exhort, encourage, and correct. No matter how wise, insightful, and knowledgeable people may be, they need the mutual accountability and affirmation featured in small groups, larger gatherings, and one-on-one conversations in the fellowship of believers. This is a crucial role of the believing community. We need the regular means to review our presuppositions, assess the validity of our observations, and compare our conclusions against the benchmark offered by Scripture and the fellowship of believers, especially those who are seasoned in the affairs of life and the marketplace. Sometimes we need correction and reorientation, and other times, affirmation.

We as readers listen in on the conversation between Qohelet and the frame narrator. We may find ourselves agreeing with Qohelet's point of view based on our own experiences and observations. We agree with Qohelet that life and work can be difficult and challenging, even raw. We find ourselves wondering about insubstantiality, transience, and foulness, the range of connotations that *hebel* features. The ideals and expectations of the job or the company or the promises of the good life fail to materialize. Our enthusiasm and good working relationships prove short-lived. Questionable ethical practices in the corporate world or suspicious management decisions leave a foul taste in our mouths. But will our discouragement and disappointment lead to bitterness and cynicism? If isolated from the sanctuary symbolized by the church, we can continue astray with our philosophy of life and work. The psalmist nearly slips into compromising his ideals because of his envy of the wicked, who prosper and seemingly lead the good life without God, until he enters the sanctuary to understand the truth (Ps 73:17). We must do the same and enter the sanctuary on a regular basis. We must balance reading Qohelet with reading the frame narrator; both voices merit a hearing.

Entering God's House

Qohelet's admonition to adopt the reverential attitude of a listener when entering the house of God (5:1–3) deserves submissive observation today. Do we enter the sanctuary ready to hear what God may say? Can we discern his voice through the speech and sharing of fellow believers assembled to worship and fellowship? Will we accept the instruction, correction, and even rebuke from others as if from God himself?

But more specifically, we need to address the role of church leaders conveying God's voice with authority. As under-shepherds, they preach, teach, disciple, mentor, and lead. The sheep should recognize their voice (John 10:3–4) and not follow a stranger, because they do not recognize his voice (John 10:5). This principle leads to two immediate implications: (1) leaders anointed by God bear a heavy responsibility of knowing God and his word and faithfully expounding and competently applying his word in order to faithfully fulfill their stewardship as under-shepherds and thereby permit God's voice to be heard; and (2) the sheep must discern God's voice through their under-shepherds and differentiate their teaching from that of false teachers who threaten to lead them astray. As sheep, marketplace members follow the under-shepherd's lead and must not be deceived into following a false shepherd. Following the genuine under-shepherd means following God's lead. Listening and responding to the true under-shepherd means hearing, discerning, and obeying God's voice. May our churches serve us well, even if they do not include marketplace-specific ministries.

Sense of Awe before God

One significant contribution the church can make is to cultivate a deep sense of awe before God, something both Qohelet and the frame narrator agree on. Since I discussed Qohelet's attitude toward God earlier, I will only summarize key points. First, Qohelet acknowledges God's sovereign authority over humanity (1:13; 2:24–26; 3:10, 18; 5:20; 6:2; 7:14; 9:1). Second, God is Creator, the source of life (5:18; 7:29; 8:15; 9:9; 11:5; 12:1, 7). Third, he holds humanity accountable and will judge them (3:15, 17; 8:12–13; 9:7; 11:9). Fourth, his ways and activities lie outside of human comprehension and interference (3:11, 14; 7:13; 8:17; 11:5). Fifth, he is the object of fear and deep reverence (5:1–7; 7:18), compelling us to keep promises and oaths before him (5:4–6; 8:2). The frame narrator reiterates Qohelet's charge to fear God (12:13) and to remember that he will judge humanity (12:14). The frame narrator's admonition to obey God's commandments (12:13) echoes Qohelet's allusion to the righteous and those who please God (2:26; 3:17; 7:26; 8:12b; 9:1–2).

But an important difference between the two men rests in Qohelet's observation that the righteous sometimes suffer the injustices of life and the wicked sometimes escape the consequences of their deeds (3:16; 7:15; 8:10, 12a, 14), and that both share a common fate (9:2). However, he bases his comments on what he sees in the world, as his refrain "under the sun/heavens" indicates (1:3, 9, 13–14; 2:3, 11, 17–20, 22; 3:1, 16; 4:1, 3, 7, 15; 5:13, 18; 6:1, 12; 8:9, 15, 17; 9:3, 6, 9, 11, 13; 10:5) and as he alludes to with similar comments (5:2; 6:5; 7:11; 11:7; 12:2). Thus, the inequality between the righteous and wicked is historical, confined to this life. Qohelet possibly hints (but may not be his understanding, given the context of 3:1–8) that a significant difference separates the righteous and the wicked—the potential of God's eschatological judgment (3:17; 8:12–13; 9:1). The frame narrator agrees with this truth (12:14).[8] The church must teach its marketplace members this important life principle and provide guidance for those struggling with injustice in the workplace.

Significantly, Qohelet seems to blame God for the bad things that happen. Somewhat philosophically, Qohelet declares: "When times are good, be happy; but when times are bad, consider this: God has made the one as well as the other. Therefore, no one can

---

8. Qohelet observes the injustices suffered by the righteous and the seeming impunity of the wicked. His observations are based on the events of this life. Based on 3:1-8 (there is a proper time for everything), then logically there will be a proper time for God to judge the righteous and the wicked (3:17). But since the timing of things in 3:1-8 alludes only to this life, then the divine judgment (3:17) may also allude only to this life. However, there is some ambiguity in interpreting 3:17: Is the point about the timing of God's judgment or is the point about God judging people on whether they maintain the proper timing in their lives? Hence, the idea of God's eschatological judgment is not overtly stated—so Qohelet may not have this understanding on eschatological judgment, whereas the frame narrator seems more clear about eschatological judgment in 12:14.

discover anything about their future" (7:14). It is uncertain whether Qohelet has in mind the good and the bad exclusively, or simply the different kinds of days in one's life. It is also unclear whether he attaches a moral aspect to the descriptors "good" and "bad." The term "crooked" in the previous verse ("Consider what God has done: Who can straighten what he has made crooked?" [7:13]) does not necessary signify moral corruption, especially in view of Qohelet's later affirmation: "This only have I found: God created mankind upright, but they have gone in search of many schemes" (7:29). In 7:13, "straight" and "crooked" are metaphors depicting what God has done. And whatever he does cannot be changed by anyone. God is upright, and his actions align with his righteous character. Humanity, on the other hand, exhibits the propensity of scheming alternative paths of conduct. Hence, I interpret "crooked" and "straight" as the possible alternative and opposite results of one's activities. The point is that whatever God does cannot be neutralized or negated—if he chooses to make something straight, it cannot be made crooked, and if he chooses to make something crooked, it cannot be straightened. This statement proclaims God's unchallengeable, sovereign authority and prerogative. Thus, "good" and "bad" days may refer more to what results in our enjoyment and satisfaction (2:24–25) and what prohibits it. God may permit us satisfying days, or he may not. Either way, the way our days proceed can determine our future. But the apparent randomness and unpredictability of how each day unfolds makes forecasting impossible.

CONCLUDING THOUGHTS

As the wisdom, counsel, and insights of Qohelet and the frame narrator provide crucial instruction and guidance for their readers, so too does the church in shepherding its members. In this role, the church needs to fulfill three major responsibilities. First, to faithfully and accurately proclaim the word of God, emphasizing Jesus Christ and him crucified, in order to nurture the flock to grow in Christ-likeness. Second, to cultivate a profound sense of the holy through corporate worship, challenging worshipers to draw close to the Lord and to abide in his presence. Third, to intentionally equip the saints for the work of service for the building up of the body of Christ (Eph 4:12) The third role's objective potentially features two distinct components: (1) equipping for the work of service—a generic, nonspecific designation of what the labor may entail—and (2) equipping for building up the body of Christ. The former component addresses all kinds of work—marketplace, domestic, and neighborhood/community. The latter deals particularly with the church. Together, they encompass the totality of one's life, responsibilities, and activities inside and outside the church.

With this understanding of its role, the church must accept a broad stewardship that oversees all aspects of its members' lives. It cannot compartmentalize without losing its integrity. It must view all of life as sacred, following Paul's mandate: "He is the one we proclaim, admonishing and teaching everyone with all wisdom, so that we may present everyone fully mature in Christ. To this end I strenuously contend with all the energy Christ so powerfully works in me" (Col 1:28–29). Believers are complete when they attain full functionality in all areas of life.

CHAPTER 7

Reflection and Recommendations

In this concluding chapter, I present my reflection and recommendations for consideration and response. Studying the wisdom book of Ecclesiastes offers another lens through which to examine the important topic of work and vocation. In this manner, I hope to add to the related literature for the benefit of marketplace readers and those who minister to them.

OUR VOCATION

Chapter 1 defines vocation as our life's work of dispensing common grace for the common good in obedience to the two greatest commandments recorded in Scripture—loving God with our all and loving our neighbor as ourselves. This comprehensive definition encompasses all of life, dispelling any dichotomization into the sacred and the secular. All areas of life and their attendant activities are sacred because God values every aspect and will submit each area to his judgment. What he regards as important, we should also in order to be faithful to our stewardship. Our pursuit of loving relationships can take different forms; it is not confined to any particular job or career trajectory. Thus, whether we are professional ministers or missionaries, white collar or blue collar, corporate employees or entrepreneurs, traditional office workers or telecommuters, housewives or househusbands, students or retirees, or working in whatever meaningfully engages us, our work should be measured by how well we care for our neighbor and how we excel in our devotion to the Lord.

Qohelet depicts four complicating factors in life—an inscrutable God, the inevitability of death, sin, and the disappointments of life—that threaten our pursuit of vocation. Since the future is beyond our control, he admonishes us to focus on the present—carpe diem. But in the present, we can still have good and bad days; there are no guarantees. The best strategy appears to be to take each day one at a time, focusing on dispensing common grace to all for the common good. Some days we may enjoy greater success than other days. That describes the vicissitudes of life, which make it difficult to maintain consistency. So long as we fear God and keep his commandments, our consciences will be clear and we can take in stride the disappointments and frustrations of the bad days. Because we have different backgrounds, training, aptitudes, giftings, and opportunities, we may fulfill our vocation in a manner that differs from that of our neighbor. We do not compare but measure ourselves according to our own particular profile.

By not softening the hard-edged aspects of life, Ecclesiastes conditions us to be resilient. Life and mission are not impossible. We may stumble, but we will not fail if we heed the admonition to fear God and keep his commandments—our whole duty in life. And his commandments are two: to love God with our whole being and love our neighbor as ourselves.

OUR CAREER AND VISION

Subsuming the traditional concept and scope of career within the grander idea of vision, we align vision with vocation. The two concepts are not identical but rather complement each other. Vision functions like a reference point by which to navigate our way through life in pursuit and fulfillment of our vocation. Clear vision keeps us on course and prevents any detours. It permits self-examination and periodic reality checks in anticipation of the final accounting before God, who will judge every deed to determine whether it is good or evil.

Reflection and Recommendations

The vicissitudes and complexities of life and the unexpected make progress difficult and unpredictable. Uncertainty may discourage and rob us of confidence. Our sense of timing in attempting to gauge our progress may or may not be all that helpful. Many parameters—our training and gifting, opportunities and circumstances, other people—can influence the advance toward our goals and objectives. But mindful of our standing with God as we fear him and keep his commandments, we exercise faith that we will complete our journey. Whereas Qohelet has a myopic view of life as he admonishes his readers to adopt his philosophy of carpe diem and its self-centeredness as the only achievable objective in life and evidences no attempt to communicate with God, we follow the frame narrator in having a broader and more farsighted vision and nurturing a personal relationship with God.

The contrast between Qohelet and the frame narrator helps us to note that Qohelet sees nothing positive about his life and work. His dissatisfaction and disillusionment stem from a desire to transcend human boundaries. Several times when he laments humanity's limitations, he immediately identifies what people can hope in: carpe diem—enjoying the momentary pleasures of life in the here and now (2:11–23 followed by 2:24–26; 3:11 followed by 3:12–13; 3:18–21 followed by 3:22; 5:16–17 followed by 5:18–20; 8:14 followed by 8:15; 9:1–6 followed by 9:7–10). The juxtaposition of the opposing pairs of verses suggests that for every negative situation (what is lamentable) there is a corresponding positive element (carpe diem). Qohelet sounds resigned to his lot and that of humanity. He and they can do no better. However, he concentrates too much on the here and now. He cannot perceive any possibility of eternal consequences for how he lives or works in this life.

The frame narrator, on the other hand, hints at something more to this life when he exhorts readers to fear God and to keep his commandments. When we strive to please God and care for others, selfish ambition fades and life can have more meaning. If we are delinquent in loving God and neighbor, we will have no compassion for others. And we may find ourselves, like Qohelet, distant from God, which prevents us from loving God. Thus, our vision ought to encompass the centrality of stewardship to God and neighbor.

PROFESSIONAL COLLEAGUES AS NEIGHBORS

Identifying professional colleagues as neighbors within the purview of honoring the second greatest commandment contributes toward embracing a more unified perspective of life as we strive to move away from a compartmentalized life orientation. In alignment with regarding all of life as sacred, we regard everyone as worthy of our sacred duty to love and to care for others. It may radicalize our approach toward work and how we relate to all the stakeholders in our corporate world. In one sense, we do not differentiate between our duties to those within our work world, our home, our church, and our community. But in another sense, we echo Paul's words: "While we have opportunity, let's do good to all people, and especially to those who are of the household of the faith" (Gal 6:10, NASB). We care for all people, but to a greater degree for those in the family of God. But as good neighbors, we must still pursue excellence as professionals in meeting corporate objectives. We strive to be valued assets in the workplace, competent and participatory team members, encouragers and even mentors to those who are struggling or less experienced, and workers who demonstrate a positive and congenial attitude and demeanor for a wholesome work environment.

With his superior wisdom, significant experience in life and work, and insightful observations, Qohelet, as the teacher, models a senior colleague in the marketplace who aspires to mentor, coach, and guide a younger coworker. He imparts knowledge and many proverbs (12:9–10). In this regard, he demonstrates care for people. His words are like goads—like embedded nails of one shepherd that sting (12:11).[1] A goad prods—sometimes painfully—the recipient to think things through and have better behavior. As noted earlier, Qohelet's words do not soften the complexities and even rawness of life. In fact, his writings make readers uncomfortable, prompting reflection and self-examination. The sting or pain motivates them to respond. An effective mentor encourages but also challenges and even rebukes if necessary.

---

1. Fox, *Time to Tear Down*, 354–55.

Reflection and Recommendations
LIFE BALANCE

Pursuing balance honors the ideal of all of life being sacred and every facet of our existence having great value. But should one area consume our time and personal resources, we struggle to maintain attentiveness to other areas. For example, work hours lengthen disproportionately, our families face a major illness or conflict, or church involvement grows heavy. Emergencies, the unexpected, accidents, and the like happen, thereby disturbing our plans and routines. Naturally, we marshal resources to address the urgent. Hopefully it is short-term. But it may be outside our ability to find a quick resolution. It becomes a protracted burden that defies easy answers. Life can quickly spiral out of control. Thus, incongruities—the topic of the next subsection— threaten to undermine our ability to attain balance. That failure in balance results in *hebel* with its triune meanings of insubstantiality, transience, and foulness. That is reality, and all we can do is to cling to our Lord in weathering the storm.

Yet, we remain mindful that balance conforms to God's will. Every aspect of our lives is important to him. Our stewardship covers all areas and not just some. He will hold us accountable. But at the same time, we cannot fret about things outside of our control. We strive to do our best and to be faithful. Indeed, balance is God's gift. We should accept it with gratitude. Ignoring the gift is tantamount to deviating from God's will.

A key characteristic of balance is maintaining the proper timing of every area of life, including work. Qohelet reinforces this idea with his sampling of contrasting pairs (3:2–8)—for example, "a time to be silent and a time to speak" (3:7b). The application to work would be "a time to toil and a time to rest." Here, "toil" can be any intentional activity and "rest" is the cessation of that activity. In our attempt to balance work and life, we normally think in terms of gainful employment versus other pursuits and responsibilities, including family and domestic duties. The statement "he has made everything beautiful in its time" (3:11a) affirms that every aspect of life has an appointed time set by God. Hence, neglecting one area because of heavy involvement in another area violates the timing imposed by God.

Qohelet's reputation as the wisest of men spurs us to gain wisdom and then exercise it in seeking and attaining balance. When he writes of carpe diem, he readily acknowledges that "satisfaction in [one's] own toil" (2:24) comes as the gift of God (2:24b–25), who also provides wisdom, knowledge, and happiness (2:26). Taking happiness and satisfaction as essentially synonymous, we see the correlation between three things God gives. Wisdom and knowledge enable us to discern the appropriate timing of things, and, in consequence, we have the potential to achieve balance and satisfaction.

INCONGRUITY

Sometimes life mystifies us, leaving us puzzled, confused, or even angry. Injustice, unmet expectations, betrayal, disappointment, unsolvable problems, inconsistencies. All these confront us as incongruities that can defy logic or reason. We feel frustrated, hurt, disappointed, or angry. Yet, it's an integral part of life, which is sometimes messy and complicated.

We draw cold comfort from reading Ecclesiastes, sympathizing with Qohelet, who laments the incongruities he encounters through personal experience and observation. In a matter-of-fact manner, he simply states each incongruity without complaining to God, unlike in the lament psalms. He appears resigned and accepting. He shows no hope that things will change for the better, since he harbors no expectations that God will intervene. And so, life continues as before (1:4–10). His only recommendation is to practice carpe diem when possible. That is the best one can do. It is God's gift, so accept and enjoy it—the one pleasure obtainable in an otherwise meaningless existence. By "meaningless," an oft-repeated motif, he connotes insubstantiality (what seems promising or substantive proves, on closer inspection, to be empty or void), transience (fleeting, temporary, vaporous), and foulness (injustice or unfairness, evil).

Yet, the fact that he writes in a forthright manner about these incongruities—hiding nothing and refusing to soften the sometimes rawness of life—conditions us readers to realize that these disturbing experiences, should we encounter them, are quite normal, shared by others. Hence, we should not mistake our struggles as God's judgment against us—as the result of our sins—or believe that we alone face these and no one else does. Ours represents a shared experience as a member of humanity in this world, under the sun.

Qohelet lives with the tension between what he expects or hopes for and the reality that falls short of his desires and dreams. Steadfastly, he prods ahead with his life and activities, not fully understanding the incongruities but accepting them as an integral part of life—giving it some thought, but not to the extent of being so distressed that he cannot function or that he accuses God of failing him in some way. He is our model to emulate. Let us acknowledge the incongruities that bother us. Let us learn to live with the resulting tension, realizing that they will never go away in this life but will stay with us. Life continues to be complex, daunting, and mysterious.

But unlike Qohelet, the frame narrator offers hope through fearing God and keeping his commandments. This stewardship lies within our ability to achieve. It speaks of a relationship where God knows what occurs in our lives, especially the incongruities. There will be a day of reckoning when he judges every deed, good or evil. He will deal decisively with every incongruity, but it will be according to his perfect timing. We acknowledge his sovereign authority by waiting on him and aligning with his timing. He will judge us by how well we live with the tension as we honor him with our reverence and obedience.

CHURCH'S ROLE

Ironically, the very institution designed to facilitate our sanctification all too often reinforces a dichotomy between the sacred and the secular. Responsibilities and activities directly connected to the church are deemed sacred—they are perceived as making a direct contribution to the kingdom. But concerns and deeds related to work or other areas of life are relegated to the secular—they are perceived as matters of this world, tainted by sin and defiling.

Seemingly, Qohelet aligns with this dichotomy by virtue of the amount of text he devotes to matters "under the sun"—concerns of this world. The motif "under the sun" occurs twenty-seven times in the first ten chapters, whereas the equivalent "under the heavens" appears an additional three times and "earth" seven more times. By contrast, he gives comparatively little attention to one's duty to God. However, he harbors a lofty regard for God, but to the point where he sees him as so transcendent and beyond human contact that Qohelet never mentions whether he himself communicates with the Lord or even tries to. The closest he comes is in 5:1–7, where he admonishes those entering the house of God to keep silent because he is in heaven and the worshiper dwells on earth. This is one-way communication—God speaks and humanity listens. Qohelet does not encourage prayer. A reverential fear, even dread, prevails.

Confirming my selection of Ecclesiastes for an investigation on work, the following related terms occur frequently: "work(er)" six times, "labor" ten times, and "toil" twenty-three times. Qohelet makes two significant points. First, work is very burdensome and difficult, to the extent that Qohelet moans that "nothing was gained under the sun" (2:11c). The following words and phrases convey this anguish: "grievous" (2:17), "despair" (2:20), "anxious striving" (2:22), "chasing after the wind" (4:6), "a grievous evil" (5:16), "miserable business" (4:8), and "the toil of fools wearies them" (10:15). And second, workers must derive some satisfaction or enjoyment from their labor (2:10, 24; 3:13, 22; 5:18–19; 8:15).

For the church to teach about the sacredness of all of life and not just a portion, it needs to recognize the challenges, difficulties, wearisomeness, anxieties, and even grief associated with the marketplace. Can its pastoral team empathize with, encourage, comfort, and commiserate with its marketplace members? At the same time, the church should acknowledge the role of work in the overall scheme, since God has assigned work as humanity's lot in life (3:22; 5:18–19; 9:9). Work represents an area of stewardship for which we all must answer to God. Will the church exhort members to persevere and remain faithful to this "calling"?

Reflection and Recommendations

From the frame narrator, we infer our broader area of stewardship: fearing God and keeping his commandments (12:13). The church, then, can fulfill its mandate to instruct and exhort its people to love God with their all and to love their neighbors as themselves. In this way, the church can foster a wholistic view of life in all its rich variety. The church can echo the frame narrator's final pronouncement: "For God will bring every deed into judgment, including every hidden thing, whether it is good or evil" (12:14). By "every deed," we infer that God will judge every area of our lives, whether in the marketplace, the home, the community at large, or social and public matters, as well as personal and private affairs. Since whatever God deems necessary to come within his purview is sacred to him, it should also be sacred to us and to the church.

The church faces a serious challenge should its members embrace Qohelet's viewpoint that life is totally *hebel*—insubstantial, transient, and foul. The threat to mental, emotional, and spiritual health rears its ugly head when someone concludes that work and life are absurd and meaningless, without lasting value. That kind of thinking approaches nihilism, where nothing holds meaning or value. But Qohelet still believes in God and in his gift of satisfaction, or enjoyment from one's labor. And because he distinguishes between righteousness and wickedness and between those who fear God and those who do not (8:12–13), he has a strong sense of morals and values that are external to himself and imposed by God—unlike existentialism. Yet, his rather matter-of-fact differentiation between the righteous and the wicked, between those who fear God and those who do not, lacks the emotive force of an admonition. He hints at the consequences without specifying the rewards and punishments and how serious they may be. And he quickly negates any possible difference in fate when he immediately follows by switching the consequences, describing how the righteous and the wicked each receive undeserving ends (8:14).

Qohelet, however, gives a much clearer picture of the satisfaction (or enjoyment) gained from one's work (or labor) in the carpe diem passages elaborated earlier. This is the only real or tangible positive outcome throughout his musings. But such benefits are short-lived and confined to the here and now. The only significant difference between Qohelet's and a humanist point of view rests in his acknowledging God as the source of any reward for work accomplished (2:24–25; 3:12–13; inferred in 3:22; 5:18–20; 8:15; 9:7).

Thus, the church should assume the role of the frame narrator in recognizing any truth or teaching from Qohelet but processing it through the lens of the final admonition to fear God and keep his commandments. Christians need to strike the proper balance between living in the moment and making the most of any given opportunity, and maintaining one's perspective of the eternal and the final judgment of God, who judges every deed as good or evil.

Bibliography

Alter, Robert. *The Wisdom Books: Job, Proverbs, and Ecclesiastes: A Translation with Commentary.* New York: W. W. Norton, 2010.
Badcock, Gary D. *The Way of Life: A Theology of Christian Vocation.* Grand Rapids: Eerdmans, 1998.
Bock, Darrell L., and Mikel Del Rosario. "The Table Briefing: Vocation, Faith, and Cultural Engagement." *BSac* 173 (2016) 235–43.
Bolden-Barrett, Valerie. "Millennials Are HR's Biggest Challenge in the Multi-Gen Workplace." HRDive, March 26, 2019. https://www.hrdive.com/news/millennials-are-hrs-biggest-challenge-in-the-multi-gen-workplace/551167/.
Brueggemann, Walter. *Theology of the Old Testament: Testimony, Dispute, Advocacy.* Minneapolis: Fortress, 1997.
Burchell, Michael, and Jennifer Robin. *The Great Workplace: How to Build It, How to Keep It, and Why It Matters.* San Francisco: Jossey-Bass, 2011.
"Challenges and Conflicts—Millennials in the Workplace." *Mining Review Africa*, June 11, 2019. https://www.miningreview.com/gold/challenges-conflicts-millennials/.
Chanos, George J. *Millennial Samurai: A Mindset for the 21st Century.* Self-Published, Amazon Digital Services, 2019. Kindle.
Crenshaw, James L. *Ecclesiastes: A Commentary.* Philadelphia: Westminster, 1987.
Danker, Frederick W. "The Pessimism of Ecclesiastes." *CTM* 22 (1951) 9–32.
Davis, John J. "The Rhetorical Use of Numbers in the Old Testament." *GJ* 8.2 (1967) 40–48.
Economy, Peter. "A New Study of 150,000 Millennials Reveals They Have 10 Surprising Things in Common." Inc., July 27, 2019. https://www.inc.com/peter-economy/a-new-study-of-150000-millennials-revealed-that-they-have-these-10-surprising-things-in-common.html.
Enns, Peter. *Ecclesiastes.* Cambridge: Eerdmans, 2011.
Foster, Craig. *My Octopus Teacher.* Directed by Pippa Ehrlich and James Reed. 1 hr. 30 mins. Netflix, 2020.
Fox, Michael V. *Qohelet and His Contradictions.* Sheffield, UK: Almond, 1989.

Bibliography

———. *A Time to Tear Down and a Time to Build Up: A Rereading of Ecclesiastes.* Grand Rapids: Eerdmans, 1999.

Fraser, Robert. *Marketplace Christianity: Discovering the Kingdom Purpose of the Marketplace.* 2nd ed. Kansas City: New Grid, 2006.

Friesen, Garry, and J. Robin Maxson. *Decision Making and the Will of God.* Colorado Springs: Multnomah, 2004.

Garber, Steven. *Visions of Vocation: Common Grace for the Common Good.* Downers Grove, IL: IVP, 2014.

Hartley, John E. *The Book of Job.* NICOT. Grand Rapids: Eerdmans, 1988.

Hatton, Peter T. H. *Contradiction in the Book of Proverbs: The Deep Waters of Counsel.* SOTSMS. Hampshire, England: Ashgate, 2008.

Hill, Alexander. *Just Business: Christian Ethics for the Marketplace.* 2nd ed. Downers Grove, IL: IVP, 2008.

Hillman, Os. *The 9 to 5 Window.* Ventura, CA: Regal, 2005.

Hunter, Lydia. "10 Unexplored Islands near Singapore Which Don't Require a Plane to Get to." The Smart Local, March 15, 2016. http://thesmartlocal.com/read/islands-getaways-singapore.

Kohll, Alan. "The Evolving Definition of Work-Life Balance." Forbes, March 27, 2018. https://www.forbes.com/sites/alankohll/2018/03/27/the-evolving-definition-of-work-life-balance/?sh=2f266489ed3e.

Kroesbergen, Hermen. "The Static Imagery of Vocation." *NZSTR* 58 (2016) 76–95.

Little, Larry. "6 Ways to Get Along with Millennials at Work." Chief Learning Officer, May 15, 2017. https://www.chieflearningofficer.com/2017/05/15/6-ways-get-along-millennials-work/.

Longman, Tremper, III. *The Book of Ecclesiastes.* The New International Commentary on the Old Testament. Grand Rapids: Eerdmans, 1998.

Marketplace Ministry. Lausanne Occasional Paper 40 (September 29 to October 5 2004). https://www.lausanne.org/content/lop/marketplace-ministry-lop-40.

McCabe, Robert V. "The Message of Ecclesiastes." *DBSJ* 1 (1996) 85–112.

Meister, Chad V., and James K. Drew, Jr., eds. *God and the Problem of Evil: Five Views.* Spectrum Multiview Books. Downers Grove, IL: IVP, 2017.

Miller, David W. *God at Work: The History and Promise of the Faith at Work Movement.* Oxford: Oxford University Press, 2007.

Miller, Douglas B. *Symbol and Rhetoric in Ecclesiastes: The Place of Hebel in Qohelet's Work.* Atlanta: SBL, 2002.

Mitchell, Helen M. "Serving Marketplace Leaders: Your Church Can Fulfill an Important Role by Supporting Businesses." *Ministry Today* 33.5 (September to October 2015) 18–24.

Ogden, Graham. *Qoheleth, Readings: A New Biblical Commentary.* Sheffield, England: Sheffield, 1987.

Petersen, Anne H. *Can't Even: How Millennials Became the Burnout Generation.* Boston: Houghton Mifflin Harcourt, 2020.

Bibliography

Schuurman, Douglas J. *Vocation: Discerning Our Callings in Life.* Grand Rapids: Eerdmans, 2004.

Schwab, Klaus. "The Fourth Industrial Revolution: What It Means, How to Respond." World Economic Forum, January 14, 2016. https://www.weforum.org/agenda/2016/01/the-fourth-industrial-revolution-what-it-means-and-how-to-respond/.

Seow, Choon-Leong. *Ecclesiastes: A New Translation with Introduction and Commentary.* AB 18C. New York: Doubleday, 1997.

Sneed, Mark R. *The Politics of Pessimism in Ecclesiastes: A Social-Science Perspective.* Ancient Israel and Its Literature 12. Atlanta: SBL, 2012.

Soo Hoo, Gilbert. "The Reality of Our Calling," *SBC HeartBeat* 260.1 (2017) 6.

Stevens, R. Paul. *The Other Six Days: Vocation, Work, and Ministry in Biblical Perspective.* Grand Rapids: Eerdmans, 1999.

Stevens, R. Paul, and Alvin Ung. *Taking Your Soul to Work: Overcoming the Nine Deadly Sins of the Workplace.* Grand Rapids: Eerdmans, 2010.

Thurrott, Stephanie. "7 Questions to Ask Yourself If You're Thinking of Making a Career Change During COVID-19." The Muse. https://www.themuse.com/advice/questions-to-ask-before-making-career-change-coronavirus.

Veith, Gene Edward, Jr. *God at Work: Your Christian Vocation in All of Life.* Wheaton: Crossway, 2002.

Watts, John D. W. "The Deuteronomic Theology." *RevExp* 74.3 (1977) 321–36.

Weeks, Stuart. *Ecclesiastes and Scepticism.* JSOTSup 541. New York: Bloomsbury, 2014.

Witherington, Ben, III. *Work: A Kingdom Perspective on Labor.* Grand Rapids: Eerdmans, 2011.

CPSIA information can be obtained
at www.ICGtesting.com
Printed in the USA
LVHW081045210922
728925LV00010B/367

9 781666 731071